The Greatest Biggest

golf

book

The Greatest Biggest

golf

book

Edited by M. P. Lannamann

Artwork by Larry Ross

Ariel Books

Andrews McMeel
Publishing

Kansas City

ʝᴧ(ᴠ(ᴙ⚋Pʝᴧ(☉(ᴧᴧ;Pᴧᴠᴙᴧᴠᴠ☉ᴧᴧʝPʝᴧᴙ(ᴧ⚋☉ᴧᴧ(ᴙᴧPᴧᴧ

www.andrewsmcmeel.com
98 99 00 01 02 BIN 10 9 8 7 6 5 4 3 2 1

Artwork by Larry Ross

This book was typeset in Sabon and Matrix by
Sally McElwain

Book design by Junie Lee

ISBN: 0-8362-6937-3
Library of Congress Catalog Card Number: 98-85183

Compiled by:

Bill Costa

Todd Kalif

Debbie Keller

Karen Liljedahl

Pat Marcello

David Payne

Nikki Stillman

Meredith Welch

Linda Wirkner

Contents

Introduction

Golf is a game of endless fascination—and endless frustration. Intense emotions of joy and despair are caused by this leisurely walk over gently rolling countryside with nothing to disturb the peace but a few friends, fourteen clubs, and a little white ball.

If you're a golf fanatic, you know how strong the pull of this much-loved game can be. Each time you play, everything seems possible. Surely next Saturday you'll make par on the sixteenth hole at the club. Or when you go on vacation—and if you can just get that chip shot right—you might equal Karrie Webb's score on the fourth at Myrtle Beach. Golf is a game in which perfection is always just out of reach.

Remember the job interview when you were asked, "What makes you get up in the morning? What motivates you?" And the only answer you could think of was an eight A.M. tee time? Well, you're not alone. Probably that interviewer was thinking the same thing! Did you check the office for the portable practice green, rolled up and slipped into the umbrella stand? For the putter cleverly planted in the ficus tree pot?

Without a doubt, golf is a game of highs and lows. You might one day agree with Lord Brabazon who said, "When I look on my life and try to decide out of what I have got most actual pleasure, I have no doubt at all in saying that I have got more

out of golf than anything else."
However, the very next day you
might find Larry Ziegler's words
more to the point: "The last time
I had this much fun, I was having
root canal."

Whatever your mood of the
moment, read on, and you'll
enjoy some of the funniest tales,
the most outrageous quotes, and
the most incredible feats of the
sport. You'll also find tips to better your game, a quiz to test your
knowledge, and information
about golf on the Internet. Enjoy!

Chapter 1

Hallowed
History

The beginnings of golf are as murky as the water hazards into which some golf balls land. Legends abound.

One is the caveman theory. A caveman wandered the hillside, swinging a knobby stick he'd found. Noticing a small pebble, he gave it a whack. He followed the stone and sent it flying again. When he swung a third time, the rock plopped into a cauldron of stew simmering over a fire. His wife was furious that he'd spoiled dinner. The caveman was intrigued. Before long, other cavemen were scurrying about the hillside in search of their own knobby sticks. The men began keeping track of how many swings it took to land a small rock into a cauldron. The rest is history.

Most historians (and all Scots) believe golf originated in Scotland. The first historical reference to the game is dated March 6, 1457. It seems King James II was afraid that the frivolous activity of golf was taking men away from practice with their bows and arrows, the primary weapon of warfare. The king warned the Scotsmen "that fut ball and golfe must be utterly cryit dune." In other words, cut it out! Fortunately, the Scots, a stubborn lot, ignored the king's decree.

In 1491, Parliament tried again to do away with golf. A law was passed that carried a fine and imprisonment for anyone caught playing the game. Property owners who allowed golf to be played on and then some. Charles was out on the links when a messenger arrived to inform him that a rebellion had broken out in his realm. A true golfer, Charles insisted on finishing out his game before attending to the uprising.

From the late 1500s until the 1920s, there were occasional clashes between religion and golf. Some clergy frowned on playing golf on Sunday. In 1900, the Women's Sabbath Alliance began a crusade against Sunday golf.

golf

As alliance president Mrs. Darwin R. James explained, forcing caddies to work on Sunday was wrong because "all criminals start on the downward path by working on Sunday."

In the early days, golf was open to all. There were no fees to pay, no starting times to book. It was a simple game, usually followed by a visit to a local tavern where "copious libations of pure and unadulterated claret" were consumed.

One of the earliest mentions of golf in America dates from 1650. According to the minutes of the upstate New York Dutch colony, a man named Jacob Jansz attacked a tavern keeper and another fellow with a golf club.

In 1659, in Fort Orange (now Albany, New York), the town fathers outlawed golf in the name of public safety. People had taken to playing golf along the streets, "which causes great damage to the windows of houses, and also exposes people to being injured."

golf

Apparently, soldiers stationed in New York during the American Revolution enjoyed a round or two of golf between battles. An ad in the *Royal Gazette* of April 21, 1779, advertised golf clubs and feather-stuffed golf balls available for "the season of this pleasant and healthy exercise now advancing." This may be the earliest record of a preseason golf sale!

Although golf was played in pockets during the 1700s and early 1800s, it didn't really catch on in the United States until John

Reid, who is often called the "Father of American Golf," got the game in motion in 1888. Reid ordered a set of golf clubs from the shop of Old Tom Morris at St. Andrews in Scotland and on February 22, 1888, he gathered a few friends together in a cow pasture in Yonkers. He laid out three short holes, using the head of one club to dig out the cups. Voilà! The first golf course in the United States.

golf

Reid and his friends ordered
more equipment from Scotland
and moved their game to a thirty-
acre plot of land. They laid out a
six-hole course over the bumpy
fields and played this course regu-
larly. They frequently
attracted spectators and
were often criticized
for playing on Sunday.
Later, they laid out
another six-hole course
in an apple orchard,
earning them the name
the "Apple Tree Gang."

On November 14, 1888, Reid proposed that the group set up an organization to regulate their newfound activity, and the St. Andrews Club of Yonkers was born.

Golf's popularity spread, and by 1894, six- and nine-hole courses had been laid out in Paterson, Lakewood, New Brunswick, and Montclair, New Jersey; Tuxedo, Newburgh, White Plains, and Long Island, New York; Newport, Rhode Island; Greenwich, Connecticut;

and Chicago, Illinois. The country's first eighteen-hole golf course was built in Chicago in 1893.

It soon became obvious that some sort of governing body was needed to establish rules, standardize play, and run tournaments. On December 22, 1894, delegates from five golf clubs met and formed the Amateur Golf Association of the United States. This later became known as the United States Golf Association.

From the beginning, members of the executive committee constantly bickered over such things as the definition of amateur and foreign players. Finally, in 1943, under the leadership of Joseph D. Dey, the committee began to work together; soon, the USGA gained the respect of both amateurs and professionals and established its lasting reputation for fairness and integrity.

The first tournament to be broadcast on national television was May's World Championship in 1953. The tournament paid ABC $32,000 to telecast the game. It wasn't long before that first deal was totally reversed; soon, networks began paying fees to the tournaments to allow them to air the events.

The number of golf courses in the United States has grown at an astounding rate. It went from fifty courses in 1895, to 1,040 in 1900, to 7,112 in 1965. By 1990, there were more than 13,000 golf courses in the United States.

golf

Chapter 2

Quips

and

Quotes

Golf combines two favorite
American pastimes: taking long
walks and hitting things with a
stick.

—P. J. O'Rourke

At least he can't cheat on his
score—because all you have to
do is look back down the fairway and count the wounded.

—Bob Hope

Eighteen holes of match or medal play will teach you more about your foe than will eighteen years of dealing with him across a desk.

—*Grantland Rice*

If you can smile when all around you have lost their heads—you must be the caddie.

—*Anonymous*

You know you're on the Senior Tour when your back goes out more than you do.

—*Bob Bruce*

Swing hard in case you hit it.
                                    —*Dan Marino*

The most exquisitely satisfying act in the world of golf is that of throwing a club. The full backswing, the delayed wrist action, the flowing follow-through, followed by that unique whirring sound, reminiscent only of a passing flock of starlings, are without parallel in sport.
                                    —*Henry Longhurst*

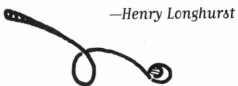

I have a tip that will take five strokes off anyone's game. It's called an eraser.

—*Arnold Palmer*

My God, he looks like he's beating a chicken.

> —*Byron Nelson*
> *(on Jack Lemmon's swing)*

Back horses or go down to Throkmorton Street and try to take it away from the Rothchilds, and I will applaud you as a shrewd and cautious financier. But to bet at golf is pure gambling.

> —*P. G. Wodehouse*

He plays just like a union man.
He negotiates the final score.

—*Bob Hope*
(*on George Meany, labor leader*)

I used to play golf with a guy
who cheated so badly that he
once had a hole in one and wrote
down zero on his scorecard.

—*Bob Bruce*

I never knew what top golf was like until I turned professional. Then it was too late.

—*Steve Melnyk*

A perfectly straight shot with a big club is a fluke.

—*Jack Nicklaus*

Golf is more fun than walking naked in a strange place, but not much.

—*Buddy Hackett*

Columbus went around the world in 1492. That isn't a lot of strokes when you consider the course.

—*Lee Trevino*

Miss a putt for two thousand dollars? Not likely!

—*Walter Hagen*

Tiger Woods? I thought that was a golf course.

> —*Sandy Lyle (on amateur golf star Tiger Woods)*

Don't hurry, don't worry . . . be sure to stop and smell the flowers.

> —*Walter Hagen*

You swing your best when you have the fewest things to think about.

> —*Bobby Jones*

I retired from competition at twenty-eight, the same age as Bobby Jones. The difference was that Jones retired because he beat everybody. I retired because I couldn't beat anybody.

—*Charles Price*

Serenity is knowing that your worst shot is still going to be pretty good.

—*Johnny Miller*

There is no movement in the golf swing so difficult that it cannot be made even more difficult by careful study and diligent practice.

—*Thomas Mulligan*

I like going there for golf. America's one vast golf course today.

—*Edward, Duke of Windsor*

Do I ever disagree with him on course strategy? Never—unless he's wrong.

—*Gary Nicklaus*
(on caddying for his father)

Man blames fate for other accidents but feels personally responsible for a hole in one.

—*Martha Beckman*

Everyone has his own choking level, a level at which he fails to play his normal golf. As you get more experienced, your choking level rises.

—*Johnny Miller*

Isn't it fun to go out on the course and lie in the sun?

—*Bob Hope*

Baffling late-life discovery: Golfers wear those awful clothes on purpose.

—*Herb Caen*

Golf is typical capitalist lunacy.

—*George Bernard Shaw*

Trent Jones must have laid this one out in a kennel.

—*Bob Rosburg (on all the doglegs at the Hazeltine, Minnesota, golf course)*

One of the nice things about the Senior Tour is that we can take a cart and cooler. If your game is not going well, you can always have a picnic.

—*Lee Trevino*

The truly great things happen
when a genius is alone. This is
true especially among golfers.

—*J. R. Coulson*

I sure was glad I ran out of holes.
I looked down at my hands and
arms to see if it was me when I
finished with the score.

—*Don January*

Golf is the only game in which a precise knowledge of the rules can earn one a reputation for bad sportsmanship.

—*Patrick Campbell*

Golf is assuredly a mystifying game. It would seem that if a person has hit a golf ball correctly a thousand times, he should be able to duplicate the performance at will. But such is certainly not the case.

—*Bobby Jones*

There are two things you can
learn by stopping your backswing at the top and checking
the position of your hands: how
many hands you have, and which
one is wearing the glove.

—*Thomas Mulligan*

The winds were
blowing fifty miles
per hour and
gusting to seventy.
I hit a par-3 with
my hat.

—*Chi Chi Rodriguez*

The player may experiment about his swing, his grip, his stance. It is only when he begins asking his caddie's advice that he is getting on dangerous ground.

—*Sir Walter Simpson*

Most golfers prepare for disaster. A good golfer prepares for success.

—*Bob Toski*

I'm the best. I just haven't played yet.

—*Muhammad Ali (on golf)*

It's a grind trying to beat sixty-year-old kids out there.

—*Sam Snead (on his decision to quit the Senior Tour at age seventy-seven)*

golf

What earthly good is golf? Life is stern and life is earnest. We live in a practical age. All around us we see foreign competition making itself unpleasant. And we spend our time playing golf! What do we get out of it? Is golf any use? That's what I'm asking you. Can you name me a single case where devotion to this pestilential pastime has done a man any practical good?

—*P. G. Wodehouse*

It took me seventeen years to get 3,000 hits in baseball. I did it in one afternoon on the golf course.

—*Hank Aaron*

I told him he was one year away from the Tour and next year he'll be two years away.

—*Chi Chi Rodriguez*

golf

It is almost impossible to remember how tragic a place the world is when one is playing golf.

—*Robert Lynd*

It would have been a hell of a ride.

—*Jack Nicklaus (on seeing an ant on top of the golf ball he was about to hit)*

Golf is a game kings and presidents play when they get tired of running countries.

—*Charles Price*

Let your hands take it away,
laddie, and feel the grass.

      —Scottish wisdom on the game

When I get out on that green
carpet called a fairway, manage
to poke the ball right down the
middle, my surroundings look
like a touch of heaven on Earth.

      —Jimmy Demaret

Chapter 3

Facts and Figures

It has been estimated that there are now more than 20 million golfers in the United States. Between one and two million new golfers join their ranks each year; of these, 60 percent are women.

If you're not a pro, the chances of making a hole in one are 1 in 12,600.

The oldest person to have a hole in one was Otto Bucher, who aced a hole in 1985 at the age of ninety-nine.

The speed at which the ball travels when hit by the average male golfer is 128 miles per hour.

In 1980, the loft on a typical 5-iron was 32 degrees; in 1997, it was 27 degrees.

The National Golf Foundation has estimated that 67 percent of business executives play golf.

According to The National Golf Foundation, the average golfer shoots in the high nineties on a par-72 course.

The universal standard for a golf ball's diameter is 1.68 inches.

A golf ball must be round and cannot weigh more than 1.62 ounces.

The record for the longest holed putt in a tournament is shared by Jack Nicklaus, who putted 110 feet in the 1964 Tournament of Champions, and Nick Price, who putted the same distance in the 1992 PGA Championship.

Forty-one percent of American golfers are members of a private or semi private golf club.

The longest drive on a standard course was made by Michael Hoke Austin, who hit a ball 515 yards in the U.S. Seniors Open Championship in 1974.

The average male golfer hits a golf ball 230 yards with a driver; a woman hits the ball 200 yards.

golf

Three players have made eight consecutive recorded birdies, a PGA record: Bob Goalby, in the fourth round of the St. Petersburg Open in 1961; Fuzzy

Zoeller, in the opening round of the 1976 Quad Cities Open; and Dewey Arnette, in the opening round of the Buick Open in 1987.

One of the most subtly difficult par-3's in the world is the twelfth hole at the Augusta National, home of the Masters. Tom Weiskopf holds the highest score for this hole, with a 13 in the 1980 Masters.

Approximately 2,800 volunteers help out at the U.S. Open each year.

In golf-crazy Japan, most golfers never play on a real golf course, since greens fees start at about $300 and membership in a golf club can cost as much as $250,000. Driving ranges are abundant, but not abundant enough: Two-hour waits to hit are not uncommon, and reservations for a tee time are often necessary.

In 1964, Tom Weiskopf won $487.50, his first earnings at the game. Since then, he has written a check for that amount to the Western Golf Association's Evans Caddie Scholarship Fund every year.

golf

The average female golfer hits the ball 140 yards with a 5-iron; a male nets 160 yards with the same club.

The first recorded hole in one was made by Tom Morris Jr. at the 1868 Open Championship.

The average golfer buys about one hundred golf balls a year.

A little more than 11 percent of Americans above the age of twelve play golf.

Chapter 4

Terrible

Lies and

Other

Stories

In 1993, Masters winner Bernhard Langer of Germany landed a ball twenty feet up in a tree while playing in a tournament in England. Langer climbed the tree and knocked the ball out. When asked what club he has used, Langer answered snappily, "A *tree* iron, of course."

Jimmy Demaret, a fun-loving pro working as a TV commentator during a Pebble Beach tournament, was asked for comment after Arnold Palmer hit a drive off the tee, over a steep cliff, and down onto the beach. As Palmer strategized, Demaret explained the obscure unplayable lie rule: "He can drop the ball behind a line not nearer the hole. His nearest point of relief in this case is Honolulu."

Lang Willie, the legendary caddie at St. Andrews who dressed in a stovepipe hat and a swallow-tail coat, was known for his sharp tongue—and his ability to drink. When a club member once accused him of being drunk on the job, Willie retorted, "Aye. But I'll get sober. T'ain't nothin' ye can do about that golf game of yours."

In the final round of the 1934 U.S. Open, Bobby Cruickshank was leading by two shots at the eleventh hole at Pennsylvania's Merion Golf Club when his 9-iron shot headed right into Baffling Brook. By some miracle, the ball hit some rocks in the streambed and bounced back onto the green. Elated, Cruikshank tossed his club in the air and started walking toward the hole. When the club came down, it hit him on top of the head. He was so shaken up that he finished third.

Alex Karras, the former tackle for the Detroit Lions, was playing once at the Red Run Golf Club in Royal Oak, Michigan. Using his considerable strength, he drove his first ball off the tee, only to watch it fly straight through the large plate glass window on the front of the clubhouse. Attempting a nonchalance which he almost certainly didn't feel, Karras put his head through the jagged hole and asked a passing waiter, "Is this room out of bounds?"

Terrible Lies and Other Stories

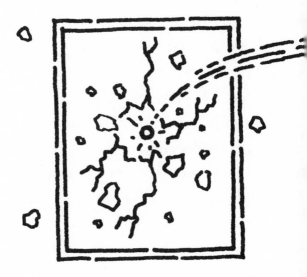

golf

Tommy Bolt was well known for his hot temper and was frequently observed throwing his clubs in exasperation. When he played one day with Arnold Palmer, he watched Palmer throw his clubs backward. Bolt, from his considerable experience, told Palmer, "You'll wear yourself out walking back to get them. You've got to throw 'em ahead of you if you want to be a professional."

Curtis Strange hit a hole in one on the twelfth at the 1988 Masters, the third ace on that hole in Masters history. Strange tossed his ball into Rae's Creek in his exuberance. A sportswriter told him later that he should have kept the ball and given it to his grandchildren. Strange answered, "I'd hoped to leave them something better than a golf ball."

During a practice round before the Masters, Sam Snead was playing with Bobby Cole, a young player from South Africa. Snead hit a long, straight drive on the dogleg thirteenth and told Cole that when he was Cole's age, he would have hit the ball right over the nearby stand of pines. Cole listened carefully, took a deep breath, and hit the ball high into the air—and right into the trees. Snead laughed and said, "Of course, those trees were a lot shorter when I was your age."

Walter Hagen had a very poor opening round in the 1920 British Open. When others who had noticed his extreme concentration asked why he was playing so hard, he responded, "I was dead scared I might finish fifty-sixth." He finished fifty-fifth.

I drove a ball into the air,
It fell to earth, I know not where;
But if I'd found it, I'll bet you,
I would have done that hole in
two!

—*Miles Bantock, 1901*

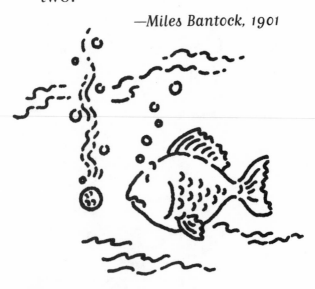

84

After astronaut Alan B. Shepard hit a golf ball on the Moon in February 1971, the Royal and Ancient Club sent him a telegram: "Warmest congratulations to all of you on your great achievement and safe return. Please refer to Rules of Golf section on etiquette, paragraph 6— 'Before leaving a bunker, player should carefully fill up all holes made by him therein.' "

Jack Nicklaus, a coleader at the 1966 Bing Crosby Pro-Am at Pebble Beach, hooked his drive at the eighteenth hole onto the beach below. As he stood with rules official George Walsh on a sand cliff trying to figure out the lie, the sand bank collapsed under Walsh, who dropped down to the beach and was swept into the Pacific Ocean.

As Walsh bobbed up and down in the gentle tide, the only thing Nicklaus could think to do was wave at him and yell, "Bon voyage!"

Tommy Aaron, in the process of shooting a 91 in the third round of the 1963 U.S. Open, began waving a white handkerchief on the ninth tee and asking, "Where do I go to surrender?"

golf

At the 1973 Heritage Classic, a wild shot by Hale Irwin flew into the gallery and landed inside a female spectator's brassiere. According to PGA rules, Irwin was required to remove the ball and drop it. The woman decided to do it herself, and Irwin avoided penalty.

During the final round of the 1919 U.S. Open, Walter Hagen managed to come from behind to create a play-off for the following day. Hagen, who was well known for his flamboyance, threw a party in his hotel room that night to celebrate. As the night wore on, a friend suggested that Hagen might like to get some sleep, commenting that Hagen's opponent had gone to bed hours before. Hagen grinned and said, "He may be in bed, but he ain't asleep."

That morning, Hagen won the play-off by a single stroke.

golf

In the early 1960s, when golf and television were still new to one another, a match between Byron Nelson and Gene Littler was being televised at Pine Valley in Clementon, New Jersey. When Nelson hit a long drive off the first tee, one of the television cameramen walked over to the ball, picked it up, and threw it back toward the tee. As Nelson stood in stupefied astonishment, the cameraman radioed back to the tee, saying, "Ask him to hit it again. We missed it."

At the eighteenth hole in the 1974 English Amateur, Nigel Denham overhit his ball, which bounced away from the green and into the clubhouse through an open door. When the ball came to rest under a table in the bar, Denham moved the table, opened a nearby window, and chipped the ball through the window and onto the green less than fifteen feet from the pin. He made the putt, thus achieving one of the most amazing pars in golf history.

golf

Even the pros turn to caddies for advice. Once, Sam Snead, when faced with a long carry over a lake, asked his caddie what he should do. The caddie replied, "Well, yesterday I caddied for Jay Hebert and he hit an 8-iron." Snead immediately pulled out his 8-iron and hit the ball, plink, right into the lake. Somewhat exasperated, Snead turned to his caddie. "You mean to tell me that Hebert hit an 8-iron from here?" he asked. "Yes, sir, he did," responded the caddie. "And he hit it into the lake, too."

Tommy Bolt, whose fine playing was matched by his fierce temper, frequently threw his clubs when he was upset. Once when he was having a particularly frustrating day at Pebble Beach, he asked his caddie for a 9-iron. The caddie handed him a 3-wood. Bolt angrily handed it back and again requested a 9-iron. When he received a 4-iron instead, he grew even angrier and asked for the 9-iron one more time. The caddie shook his head and told Bolt, "These two are all that's left in your bag."

During the 1980 Inverary Classic, Curtis Strange was crossing a small bridge over a stream when his caddie was jostled by passing spectators. With a fifty-pound bag on his shoulder, the caddie lost his balance and veered toward the water. Strange kept the caddie from falling by grabbing his arm, but the golf bag tilted and dumped most of Strange's clubs into the stream, causing Strange to play the rest of the tournament with a 2-iron, a 3-iron, a 5-iron, and a putter.

When Davis Love III was playing with Lee Trevino in the PGA Championship, his nerves made it hard to concentrate. He said to Trevino, "If it's all the same to you, I don't think I'll do much talking." Trevino, famous for his nonstop con-versation, replied, "That's okay, Davis. All you have to do is to listen. I'll do enough talking for both of us."

golf

Joyce Wethered, winner of four British Women's Championships and five British Women's Opens, had amazing powers of concentration. When she was about to putt during a 1920 tournament, a train went by, making a terrible racket. Wethered went right ahead and made the putt. When she was asked later whether the train had bothered her, she replied, "What train?"

On the final hole of the 1929 Ryder Cup at Moortown, near London, American Joe Turnesa hooked a shot behind the club-house marquee. Taking the next shot, Johnny Farrell pitched the ball back over the marquee to the green, only four feet from the pin—and Turnesa sank the easy putt.

golf

On the ninth hole of the 1964 Australian Wills Masters, Arnold Palmer's second shot lodged in the fork of a gum tree. Palmer climbed to the ball, twenty feet from the ground, hit the ball thirty yards with the "back" of his golf club, and two strokes later had sunk his putt.

W. C. Fields was such a golf enthusiast that he bought a home adjacent to a golf course. However, he was incensed by the geese that frequented the water hazard nearby and was reported to have charged at a flock of them, dressed in a bathrobe and brandishing a towel, shouting, "Either poop green or get off my lawn!"

golf

Chapter 5

First
Courses

Royal Melbourne, Australia

Playing golf at Royal Melbourne can be like stepping onto the set of a Hollywood movie. Men wearing ascots and crested blazers wait their turn, while women in flowing tartan skirts float by. There are no carts, no caddies. And even in the heat of summer, men in shorts must wear kneesocks.

Royal Melbourne, on Australia's tranquil southern coast, is considered by some to be the world's finest golf club. Most of the fame belongs to the West Course, designed in 1926 by Alister Mackenzie, genius golf-course architect. The East Course, designed in 1932 by Alex Russell, is less distinguished but no less of a challenge. For tournaments, a composite course is created with twelve holes from the West, six holes from the East, and no road crossings.

No matter which course you play, you'll find both courses are exquisitely beautiful, extremely challenging, with a fabulous Australian setting.

Jasper Park Lodge, Canada

With rocky cliffs and snow-capped peaks towering over the valley, turquoise-blue glacial waters riffling down creek beds, and elk, moose, and occasional bears strolling along the road-way, Jasper Park in the Canadian Rockies is one of the most breathtaking places on Earth. The golf is breathtaking too.

Set on the majestic glacial shores of Lac Beauvert, Jasper Park Lodge was ingeniously

designed by Stanley Thompson
to blend with its awesome surroundings. The course opened in
1925 to worldwide acclaim, and
today is an international favorite.

If you can manage to keep
from gazing too long at the
extraordinary beauty around
you, you'll be amply rewarded.
Jasper Park can be as challenging
to play as it is spectacular to
look at. The toughest hole (nine)
is a narrow green lined with trees
on one side and bunkers on the
other. Hope the wind doesn't
blow when you play it!

golf

Royal Lytham and St. Anne's, England

There's a plaque in the rough on the seventeenth hole of Royal Lytham and St. Anne's commemorating Bobby Jones's brilliant shot there and his first British Open victory. On summer evenings, members gather on seventeen to try their own strokes of genius.

Designed by George Lowe Jr. and Charles Hawtree in 1897, this course has had a long association with the best of golf. Its list of

Open winners reads like a *Who's Who* in international golf: Bobby Jones (1926), Peter Thomson (1958), Bob Charles (1963), Tony Jacklin (1969), Gary Player (1974), Seve Ballesteros (1979), Tom Lehman (1996).

Other than having eighteen holes, Royal Lytham and St. Anne's is like no other golf course and makes a lasting impression on those who play there. Its most unusual holes are eight through ten, which are surrounded by shops, houses, and townsfolk going about their business.

Royal St. George's, England

The sky is usually gray and the wind frequently whips in from the rim of the English Channel. But when you're playing Royal St. George's, the course is so prestigious and the setting so lovely that the weather hardly matters.

Royal St. George's is southern English golf at its most aristocratic. You must have a handicap of no higher than 18 to play here. And though it's a men's club, women are allowed if their handicap is low enough.

Designed by Dr. Laidlaw Purvis in 1887, Royal St. George's is a dramatic course, with undulating terrain, high dunes, massive bunkers, and challenges galore. The British Open has been played here twelve times, most recently in 1993, when Greg Norman claimed the championship.

One of the benefits of playing here is that the Eurotunnel is within driving distance. You can cap off your day on the green with an elegant evening in France.

golf

Sunningdale, England

Sunningdale is like a jewel in the English countryside. Wide, emerald greens, gently rolling fairways, and towering pines mark the club, which itself is nestled among spectacular mansions hiding behind high stone walls—all just an hour's drive from London.

Though London golf is notoriously upscale, the climate at Sunningdale can be warm and familiar. Willie Park Jr. was the Old Course designer; the New

Course was originally designed by H. S. Colt in 1922, and revised by Tom Simpson in 1935 and Ken Cotton in the 1950s.

Fame first touched Sunningdale in 1926, when Bobby Jones scored a "perfect" round of 66 in a British Open qualifier. Since then, the Old Course has often been rated the second-best inland course in Britain.

Ballybunion, Ireland

The bridge at Ballybunion stretches across the ocean, barely visible through the haze. At times, a woman stands there selling her wares, but if you see this murky vision, look away, or you will die in seven years.

Or so the legend goes.

Ireland's west coast is steeped in legend and lore, and the courses at Ballybunion are no different. There's a graveyard haunting the first tee of the Old Course, and the fourth is so hidden that without a caddie a new visitor can easily get lost.

Still, the golf at Ballybunion is some of the best in the world. The Old Course hangs over the ocean, drops down to the beach at the seventeenth hole, and rises up again, cutting a narrow passage through the dunes. The Cashen Course is already a modern classic.

Since Irish golf is relaxed and unhurried, go ahead and linger. You'll want to savor Ballybunion for as long as you can.

Carnoustie Links, Scotland

The rugged northeast coast of Scotland is cold and windy. There you'll find the castles Slains (the inspiration for *Dracula*) and Craigievar (a model for Disneyland), the world-famous distilleries of Glenfiddich and Glenlivet, and world-class golf at Carnoustie.

Carnoustie was first designed in 1842 by Allan Robertson, then revised in 1867 by Old Tom Morris, and revised again in

1926 by James Braid, with a few slight changes since. Nearly 7,000 yards long, Carnoustie can prove difficult even on a good day. Site of the 1999 British Open, Carnoustie has previously hosted the championship five times.

To many, Carnoustie defines Scottish golf: historic links at a seaside resort, a constant wind in your hair, dune ridges, sand hills, flaming gorse bushes, and green grasses that look greener when it rains—which it does with great unpredictability.

Prestwick, Scotland

About every ten minutes a train rumbles past on the right. On the left is a jumble of hip-high rough, unplayable even for champions. And in the middle is Prestwick's first tee—one of the world's most infamous openings.

Like many Scottish courses, Prestwick is ripe with antiquity. The Cardinal Bunker on the third tee has been in play for 130 years. And the famous seventeenth hole (known as "The

Alps") is the same as it was in 1860, when Willie Park Sr. won the first British Open.

The landscape at Prestwick is truly remarkable. You can watch boats sail the Firth of Clyde, gaze at the mountains on the Arran Islands, and marvel at Ailsa Craig—an enormous, round rock rising from the sea—all of which can make waiting your turn a memorable event in itself.

golf

Royal Troon, Scotland

The Postage Stamp, as Royal Troon's number eight is known, is a model for modern golf-course design. Its tiny green is its principal difficulty, especially on a windy day—which most days are at Royal Troon.

Though the two courses at Royal Troon were designed by the same architect, their play is very different. The Champion Course (designed by Willie Fernie, 1900) is longer, more treacherous, and significantly more complex than the Portland Course (designed by Willie Fernie and Charles Hunter, 1905). Still, the Portland course is challenging enough to be used for qualifying rounds when Royal Troon hosts the British Open, as it often has.

Of all the great holes at Royal Troon, the eighteenth is the most dramatic. Finishing in front of the clubhouse windows, you might feel like Arnold Palmer winning the British Open with a flourish.

St. Andrews, Scotland

High drama is the only way to describe St. Andrews. There are seven extraordinary courses in this east coast town, though the most acclaimed is the Old Course, which dates back to the beginning of the fifteenth century.

Though the Old Course was founded in about 1400, its present design is credited to Old Tom Morris. It's one of—if not the—most famous courses in the world, and the atmosphere here is completely international. Before your game is over, you're likely to have heard as many languages as at an Olympic event.

Besides its astonishing history, incomparable grandeur, international acclaim, and dramatic first and eighteenth holes (which are almost always played to a crowd), the Old Course is most famous for hole seventeen, the Road Hole. It's arguably the most famous hole in golf (and will likely be one you'll remember for a lifetime, no matter how you played it).

The American Club, Wisconsin

Surrounded by an 800-acre nature sanctuary on the edge of Lake Michigan, the austere beauty of Wisconsin's American Club will have you planning your next trip back.

The three courses at the Blackwolf Run complex (American Club is the name of the resort's historic hotel) were designed by the amazing Pete Dye. The River Course (1990) is a roller coaster, twisting past forests, over glacial hills, and crossing the Sheboygan River again and again. You'll want to linger on the panoramic Meadow Valley Course (1988) and marvel at the railroad-car-turned-bridge. Whistling Straits is a walking-only course, like the best Scottish links.

The decade-old American Club has been one of golf's best-kept secrets. But with the 1998 U.S. Women's Open held here, the news will surely spread.

Augusta National, Georgia

Augusta National, home of the Masters since 1934, is surely one of the most beautiful golf courses in the world. The 385-acre site was once a nursery, which may explain the splendor of the flowers, azaleas, and magnificent tall pines that line the fairways.

The course, inspired by Bobby Jones and his friend Clifford Roberts, was designed by Alister Mackenzie and completed in 1931. Water—several lakes and the famous Rae's Creek—contributes to the difficulty of the course. Many hopefuls have come to grief in the lake at the end of the sixteenth. Holes eleven, twelve, and thirteen, which run along the creek and have water directly adjacent to their greens, have been given the nickname "Amen Corner."

In addition, the greens throughout the course have unexpected twists and rolls and are some of the fastest in the world. No wonder so many great dramas have been played out here!

The Broadmoor, Colorado

High in the foothills of the eastern Colorado Rockies, the Broadmoor basks in three hundred days of sunshine each year. With masterful courses and unparalleled scenery, it's golf at its best.

There are three courses at the Broadmoor, each one challenging and different. The old and famous East Course is probably responsible for the Broadmoor's "Riviera of the Rockies" reputation.

Designed by Donald Ross in 1918, the East Course is marked by lush fairways, fast greens, pines, oaks, and glistening ponds.

Robert Trent Jones Sr. designed the West Course (1950 and 1965). Typical of a Jones design, it's remarkably difficult, bringing you high into the foothills, then down to earth again. And if that's not enough, Arnold Palmer and Ed Seay employed eighty-nine bunkers on their sweeping Mountain Course (1976), which averages out to five per hole.

The Boulders, Arizona

The Arizona desert is like nothing else on Earth. And the Boulders sits in the heart of it. Gila monsters, roadrunners, and rattle snakes often lounge in what little shade there is, watching as you take aim at the long spines of a giant saguaro cactus—the only green marker in sight.

Once upon a time, golf—even in this arid countryside—was always lush, green, and wet. But along came Jay Morrish, with a deep respect for the desert environment. He built a course that is a perfect blend of golf and desert, fairways and bobcats, holes perched atop boulder formations, and naturalized cacti springing up in sand bunkers.

Balls in the rough are lost forever; balls in the dry desert air just soar. Canyons and ravines are part of the game here, along with cottontails and quail. Even on an off day, golf at the Boulders is unforgettable.

golf

Grand Cypress, Florida

Deftly designed by Jack Nicklaus, there's something for everyone at Grand Cypress, including the LPGA, whose Tournament of Champions was hosted here through 1996.

The East Course (1988) provides majesty and challenge in just nine holes. The beauty of the North-South Course (1986) belies its treachery. The fairways are lined with tall, grassy mounds; the shimmering lake comes into play on thirteen of its eighteen holes.

The New Course (1988) is the most fun to play. It's a masterful replica of St. Andrews, complete with a meandering stream, stone bridge, and faux Road Hole.

The Greenbrier, West Virginia

You can see his famous pink shirt from a mile away. His pants are pressed, his black shoes shine, and he's always wearing his trademark straw hat. Sam Snead, Greenbrier's "golf professional emeritus," reigns here.

In the beautiful valley of White Sulfur Springs, West Virginia, lies Greenbrier's three acclaimed courses. The masterful Old White Course, designed by Charles Blair Macdonald in 1913, has a decidedly Scottish flavor. It makes fantastic use of its natural valley contours, and the crowd that gathers around hole one rivals that of St. Andrews.

The Lakeside Course (designed by Dick Wilson in 1963) couldn't be more beautiful, nor the Greenbrier Course (designed by Jack Nicklaus in 1978) more brutal—it has hosted the Solheim Cup and Ryder Cup for good reason. Just finishing the Greenbrier Course is an accomplishment to write home about.

Mauna Kea, Hawaii

The northeast side of the island of Hawaii looks more like the surface of another planet than a tropical Pacific island, where acres of sharp black lava rock outline the emerald fairways of legendary golf courses like Mauna Kea.

Robert Trent Jones Sr. designed Mauna Kea in 1965, and it's still considered the jewel of the Pacific. A string of par-3s takes you past the jungle, over an ocean inlet, down to the

Kohala coast beach, and back to a bunkered green.

But the real challenge at Mauna Kea may be keeping your mind on golf. The panorama of the vast Pacific, the exotic scent of tropical flowers, and the warm Hawaiian breeze will all compete for your attention. If you want to make the most of your game at Mauna Kea, don't keep your eye on the ball.

Pasatiempo, California

The optical illusions you'll find at Pasatiempo make playing a magical mystery. Fairways that look like a sliver from a distance are actually quite wide; ravines that appear a stone's throw away are actually quite far. The intimidating par-5 first hole may turn out to be the easiest to play.

The genius of Pasatiempo is pure Alister Mackenzie. The course is just an hour south of San Francisco, but you'd never know it, with the eucalyptus and cypress trees towering over you and the deep blue Pacific shimmering in the distance.

Mackenzie designed Pasatiempo in 1929, and some say it was closest to his heart. (He lived just off the sixth fairway.) It's a lovely course, surrounded by forests and checkered with ravines and gullies. Packed with Mackenzie's visual tricks, it will keep you on your toes from start to finish.

golf

Pebble Beach, California

California's Monterey Peninsula is as dripping in fame as it can be in coastal fog. Here's where John Steinbeck wrote *Cannery Row,* Edward Weston photographed sensuous sand dunes, and twenty-one-year-old Jack Nicklaus won the U.S. Amateur Championship at Pebble Beach.

Designed by Jack Neville and Douglas Grant, Pebble Beach opened in 1919 and quickly captured America's heart. It has been written about, photographed, and painted more than any other American golf course. Nearly every hole is famous, and the legendary sequence of holes six through ten might leave you telling stories for years.

It's just about impossible to have a bad day at Pebble Beach. Below the coastal bluffs, the Pacific pounds the rocky shore, seals sun themselves, and pelicans dive for lunch. Pebble Beach is California golf—and the California coast—at its absolute best.

golf

Pinehurst, North Carolina

The Sandhills of North Carolina are rich with southern charm, local history, pine forests, and 144 holes of golf. Fortunately, holding the title of the world's largest golf resort hasn't affected the quality of play at Pinehurst. After nearly a hundred years, it's still one of America's golf meccas.

Pinehurst was made famous by its course Number 2, an extraordinary course designed by Donald Ross in 1907 and still the region's premier layout. Its closest rival is the new Number 8, masterfully designed by Tom Fazio in 1996 with a profound respect for the towering pines and natural wetlands that surround the area. It's challenging enough to host the 1999 U.S. Open and beautiful enough to make you want to play at a leisurely southern pace.

golf

Spanish Bay, California

Like the best of Scottish links, the Links at Spanish Bay is masterfully bathed in just two colors: the grayish green of seaside fairways and the bright white of California's sand dunes.

The Links at Spanish Bay was designed in 1988 by an almost unbelievable partnership of Robert Trent Jones Jr., Tom Watson (five-time British Open champion), and Sandy Tatum (former USGA president). It's an amazingly Scottish course, with fantastic ocean views, hip-high rough, imposing sand dunes, and almost constant wind.

Your game is likely to start with terror—the opening hole at Spanish Bay is one of the toughest on the Monterey Peninsula. The course will take you from the shores of the Pacific, through a seaside forest, then back to the beach—and into the wind!—for a six-hole finish you'll never forget.

golf

Winged Foot, New York

Seven of Winged Foot's par-4s are more than 440 yards long, which makes playing this course a challenge for the best of players. Jack Nicklaus maintains that the seventeenth hole, with its narrow drive through trees and its green protected by bunkers, provides one of the greatest tests of a golfer's skill.

The two Winged Foot courses, East and West, were designed by A. W. Tillinghas and completed in

1923. Although the longer West Course is the one used for championship golf, the East Course remains the favorite of many players.

Four U.S. Opens have been played here, which were won by golf greats Bobby Jones (1929), Billy Casper (1959), Hale Irwin (1974), and Fuzzy Zoeller (1984). Winged Foot is named after the emblem of the New York Athletic Club, whose members were among the founders of the course.

golf

Chapter 6

Links

Legends

Seve Ballesteros

As a nineteen-year-old in 1976, Seve Ballesteros tied for second in the British Open at Royal Birkdale. That same season, he was the youngest golfer to win the European Tour's Vardon Trophy for low scoring average.

In 1976, Ballesteros led the European money list and won the Dutch Open. In 1986, he was the first player to win more than $1 million and £1 million in career earnings.

Born in Pedrena in northern

Spain, Ballesteros learned to play golf as a six-year-old by hitting balls in fields on his father's farm. He had one club—a 3-iron.

Ballesteros's early versatility with his limited equipment enabled him to extricate himself from some difficult situations as an adult. In the 1979 British Open, he hit a shot into a parking lot next to the course at Royal Lytham. He recovered to fifteen feet and birdied. That won him his first major title and made him the first continental European to win the Open in seventy-two years.

Patty Berg

Patty Berg, born in 1918 in Minneapolis, didn't let her five-foot-one stature keep her from competing in golf—or football. She was quarterback on the neighborhood boys' team, the "Fiftieth Street Tigers." She began playing golf at thirteen and won her first tournament three years later.

Berg served in the U.S. Marine Corps Reserve during World War II and returned to playing pro golf in 1946. By

1958, she had earned a record fifteen major championships. In her lifetime, she earned eighty-four titles.

In 1949, Berg, Babe Didrikson, George Zaharias, and Fred Corcoran formed the Ladies Professional Golf Association. In 1951, Berg was one of the first four women honored in the LPGA Hall of Fame.

golf

Jo Anne Carner

One of the greatest woman golfers of the modern era, Jo Anne Carner is known for hitting long, consistent drives and for going into contortions when she misses a putt. She plays enthusiastically, attacking the golf course with power and determination.

Carner won five U.S. Amateur Championship titles, in 1957, 1960, 1962, 1966, and 1968, before turning pro in 1970 at the age of thirty. Since then, she has won thirty-nine tournaments, more than any other woman golfer in history.

Nicknamed "Big Momma," Carner's friendly, easygoing nature made her a role model for other women on the Tour. She won the U.S. Open in 1971 and 1976, and came close to winning it again in 1987 when she lost in a three-way play-off to Laura Davies. She was named the tenth member of the LPGA Hall of Fame.

Nick Faldo

Nick Faldo's interest in golf began when he watched Jack Nicklaus play in a Masters on television in 1971. "I just remember watching him hit the ball and thinking, I'd like a go at this."

At six-foot-three and 195 pounds, Faldo is tall for golfing, a sport where most players are average size or smaller. However, his size has never seemed to be a problem. In 1987, Faldo won the British Open and then won two more British Opens and three

Masters within five years.

In mid-career, Nick Faldo turned to golf instructor David Leadbetter to help him recraft his swing. They examined the swing from all angles and broke it down into mechanical steps, then rebuilt it to give Faldo his winning style.

In 1992, Faldo met Ben Hogan, then eighty-three. He asked Hogan to autograph a copy of Hogan's book, *Five Lessons: The Modern Fundamentals of Golf,* the first golf book Faldo had been given.

Walter Hagen

Walter Hagen was a confident twenty when he first appeared in American golf in 1913. Considered brilliant in his short game and at putting, Hagen brought a mental understanding to the game that undermined many of his opponents. His confidence, aggressive style of golf, and ability to extricate himself from trouble endeared him to fans.

Hagen, known as "the Haig," won two U.S. Opens, four British Opens, and the Canadian and

French Opens once each from 1914 to 1931. He also won five PGA finals in the 1920s and captained the Ryder Cup team from 1927 to 1939.

Hagen's fans remember him as larger than life with a great sense of humor. His flamboyant ways and great sense of showmanship made him a constant favorite with the crowds. Hagen is quoted as saying: "Never hurry, never worry, and don't forget to stop and smell the flowers along the way."

Ben Hogan

Ben Hogan was devoted to perfection. His strategy was to learn a course inch by inch and plan the best routes for each hole. "Management is 80 percent of winning," he said.

Between 1948 and 1957, Hogan won four U.S. Opens, two Masters, one British Open, and a second PGA (his first was in 1946). Only three other golfers have also won four U.S. Opens: Willie Anderson, Bobby Jones, and Jack Nicklaus.

Hogan was seriously injured when a bus ran into the car he was driving with his wife, Valerie, in 1949. Although he was told he would never walk again, he entered the Los Angeles Open the following year and tied with Sam Snead, who won the play-off. That summer, legs bandaged and in too much pain to pick up the ball from the cup, he scored a 74 to force a U.S. Open play-off with Lloyd Mangrum and George Fazio. He stroked a 69, beating them both in one of the most emotional play-offs in golfing history.

Bobby Jones

Robert Tyre Jones Jr. stunned the golf world by winning the British Open, the British Amateur, the U.S. Amateur, and the U.S. Open all in the year 1930, thus winning the Grand Slam. He was the first and only golfer to do so.

Bobby Jones played his entire career as an amateur. He golfed only a few months each year. The rest of his time he studied engineering at Georgia Tech, then literature at Harvard, and law at Emory. He later practiced law in his native city of Atlanta.

Jones won the U.S. Open at Minneapolis by sinking a forty-foot putt with his putter, "Calamity Jane"—an amazing shot under the circumstances.

Jones had a hair-trigger temper and a reputation for high standards. He managed to overcome the first, but his dedication to his principles cost him the 1925 U.S. Open to Willie McFarlane of Scotland. Jones insisted his ball moved after address and demanded a 1-stroke penalty on himself.

Nancy Lopez

Nancy Lopez began playing golf as an amateur in the 1970s. Her friendly personality and infectious smile made her a great favorite with the public and brought the women's game significantly more media prominence. Her swing fails to follow the classic style, but who would want to change it—it works!

The world was Lopez's golfing green in 1978, when she had eight wins, with a record five in a row. She earned the Vare Trophy

for the low scoring average that
year and again in 1979. In 1978,
she was also named LPGA
Rookie of the Year and LPGA
Player of the Year. In 1987,
Lopez was inducted into the
LPGA Hall of Fame, the

youngest player
ever to achieve
that honor.

Charles Blair Macdonald

Charles Blair Macdonald, born in Chicago in 1856, fell in love with golf when he went to Scotland to attend university. His grandfather took him to Old Tom Morris's shop for handmade clubs and lessons.

Although Macdonald was a fine player, he is remembered most for his passion for the game, his conviction that the game should use the 1754 rules developed in Scotland, and his superb abiltities as a golf-course architect. He designed the first eighteen-hole golf course in the United States, which opened in Wheaton, Illinois, in 1893.

Macdonald designed the National Golf Links of America (1911) in Southampton, New York, the first great golf course in the United States. Other courses he designed are the Mid-Ocean Club in Bermuda (1924), the Yale University golf course in Connecticut (1926), and the Old White Course, in West Virginia (1914).

Tom Morris Sr.

Old Tom Morris, who won four British Open titles, is considered the first of the great names in championship golf. He also worked as a cleemaker (club maker) and resident golf professional for the Royal and Ancient Golf Club of St. Andrews in Scotland during the 1880s. Morris's clubs and balls were used in 1888 by John Reid, who founded the St. Andrews Golf Club in Yonkers, New

York, the first in the United States.

Morris welcomed another American to the sport, Charles Blair Macdonald, when he came for equipment and lessons in 1872. Macdonald was responsible for introducing golf to the U.S. Midwest in the 1890s.

golf

Tom Morris Jr.

Young Tom Morris of St. Andrews, Scotland, is considered by some to be the finest golfer who ever lived. He turned professional when he was fourteen, and won the British Open when he was seventeen—the youngest to do so. By the time he turned twenty, he had won four titles.

He played during the time when the featherie (the earlier ball, which was a leather sac stuffed with feathers) was replaced by the sturdier gutta-

percha ball, and thus was one of
the earliest pros to use irons
more than wooden clubs.
Previously, irons had been used
sparingly because they damaged
the featherie.

Unfortunately, Morris died at
the age of twenty-four after
becoming extremely depressed
when his wife and baby died in
childbirth. Had he lived longer,
he would no doubt have amassed
a greater number of titles; his
early death was a great loss to
the game.

Byron Nelson

Most people think of a "little black book" as a list of names and telephone numbers of potential dates for an evening. But Byron Nelson kept track of his golf in a little black book. By consulting it, he identified his flaws and then corrected them.

Nelson had a good eye for golf. He began to learn how to play by working as a caddie at the Glen Garden Country Club in Fort Worth, Texas.

"Iron Byron" played for U.S.

war bonds in 1944 and 1945, swinging his way to repeated victories. In 1945, he won eighteen golf tournaments, including eleven in a row, with a stroke average of 68, an all-time low.

Some say Nelson was at a disadvantage playing thirty-six holes in one day because his drive was so straight that he would drive into the divots he made on the first eighteen. Others say, in a more serious vein, that Nelson was probably the most consistent American player ever.

Jack Nicklaus

Since becoming a pro in 1961, Jack Nicklaus has won eighteen major championships, including six Masters, five PGA Championships, four U.S. Opens, and three British Opens. He has won fifty-six PGA tournaments and fifteen foreign events, and is generally considered the finest golfer of the modern era.

Nicklaus, nicknamed the "Golden Bear" by his many fans, wasn't the first player to win $1 million in career earnings, but he was the first to win $2 million, $3 million, and $4 million.

Considered the "Master" of Augusta for his amazing six wins there, Nicklaus gave his fans a thrill in 1998 by playing in his fortieth Masters at the age of fifty-eight—and finishing in the top ten!

Nicklaus not only knows how to whack a golf ball, he also knows how to lay out courses. He has developed a second career designing golf courses; one of recent his commissions is to renovate the Old Course at St. Andrews in Scotland.

Greg Norman

As a boy, Greg Norman caddied for his mother in his native Brisbane, Australia. He fell in love with the game, and his mother bought him two Jack Nicklaus instructional books, *55 Ways to Play Golf* and *Golf My Way*.

Norman won twenty-nine tournaments around the world—mostly in Europe and Australia—before he joined the American circuit full-time in 1984.

In 1986, Norman won his first British Open at Turnberry,

Scotland, with an exceptional 63 in what sportswriter John Feinstein called near hurricane conditions. That year he was ahead in each of the other major tournaments, only to lose in the final round. His only other major came in 1993, when he won the British Open.

"The Great White Shark," as Norman is known, is admired for his long, straight drives and easy rapport with the audience. His nickname reflects his blond hair and his interest in deep-sea fishing.

Arnold Palmer

Arnold Palmer's popular playing gave golf a big boost, helping to create audiences for the game on the new television screen in the 1950s. Palmer joined champions Jack Nicklaus and Gary Player to form golf's Big Three in the 1950s and 1960s. They won tournaments—and admirers— all over the world.

"Arnie's Army," his cohort of loyal fans, loved his daring, powerful approach to golf. When Palmer displayed his strong emotions—

despair or triumph—his fans suffered and celebrated with him.

Between 1958 and 1964, Palmer won seven of the twenty-five majors in which he competed. From 1958 to 1967, he won forty-four Tour events, two British Opens, and one Australian Open.

Today, the golfer who wins the most money on Tour earns the Arnold Palmer Award. The award recognizes that Palmer's enormous popularity is largely responsible for the tremendous boom in the sport.

golf

Gary Player

Gary Player of South Africa stole Arnold Palmer's thunder by winning the Masters in 1961. His popularity peaked in 1965 when he won the U.S. Open. He was the first foreign player to win that event in forty-five years. Player earned more acclaim when he donated the $25,000 purse to cancer research and to junior golf.

The South African tied with Ben Hogan in winning nine major championships. Only Jack

Nicklaus, Bobby Jones, and
Walter Hagen have won more.

Player, Arnold Palmer, and
Jack Nicklaus were known as the
"Big Three" in the 1960s. During
his career, Player has won
three Masters (1961,
1974, 1978), two
PGA Championships
(1962 and 1972),
one U.S. Open
(1965), and
three British
Opens (1959,
1968, 1974).

Gene Sarazen

Gene Sarazen won the U.S. Open in 1922 when he was only twenty years old. The next year, Sarazen, known as "the Squire," beat the popular Walter Hagen for the PGA title. "The Haig" retaliated, beating Sarazen in a 1927 exhibition game.

Sarazen applied flying lessons to golf. After learning about the principle of "lift" for flying an airplane from Howard Hughes, Sarazen developed a "sand wedge" club to blast balls out of the sand.

Sarazen's sand wedge helped bring him victory in the U.S. Open and British Open, both in 1932. At the time, he was the only man besides Bobby Jones to win both tournaments in the same year. In 1935, he won the Masters—after amazing the crowd by holing a 220-yard shot at the fifteenth hole for a double eagle.

Sam Snead

Sam Snead learned to play golf barefoot as a boy in the Allegheny Mountains in Virginia. When he hit the golf circuit in 1936 as a twenty-four-year-old, his easy, natural swing and his southern drawl made him an immediate favorite with the spectators.

For more than fifty years, Snead has been one of the most popular players in the United States. Included in his record

number of wins are three
Masters, three PGA champi-
onships, and one British Open.
He was never able to win the
U.S. Open, although he was
runner-up four times.

Snead's powerful drive and
smooth swing earned him the
nickname "Slammin' Sammy." In
1965, when Snead was fifty-
three, he won the Greensboro
Open, the oldest man ever to win
a regular PGA tournament. In
1980, at sixty-eight, he joined the
PGA Senior Tour.

Annika Sorenstam

Annika Sorenstam, who was born in Sweden, attended the University of Arizona and won seven collegiate titles while a student there. In 1991 she was both the NCAA champion and the College Player of the Year.

In 1992 Sorenstam won the World Amateur Championship. She turned pro and played on the WGP European Tour the following year, earning the Rookie of the Year title. She soon began playing on the LPGA Tour, and won the U.S. Women's Open in 1995 and 1996.

A popular player and a hard worker, Sorenstam explains to her fans, "On any given day I may hit balls for one-third my time, putt the same, and hit nine holes."

Sorenstam is the first foreign-born woman to win the Vare Trophy for the low scoring average, which she did in 1995 and 1996. She was also named LPGA Player of the Year in 1997.

Lee Trevino

Lee Trevino, the son of a Mexican gravedigger, stormed out of Texas and hit the golf circuit in 1967. He was one of a series of famous professional golfers from the second-biggest state in the Union. He won the U.S. Open in 1968, with four rounds in the 60s.

Trevino won the U.S. Open again in 1971, and the British Open in 1971 and 1972. He was only the fourth man to win the

U.S. and British Opens in the same year.

Trevino, a real character, brings a true sense of fun to the game. Breaking tradition with most professional golfers who preceded him, Trevino loves to talk on the course. He chatters incessantly with his fans, who love him. His followers are known as "Lee's Fleas."

Harry Vardon

Harry Vardon was the leading British professional golfer in the 1890s, 1900s, and 1910s. Along with James Braid and John Henry Taylor, he was part of the Great Triumvirate of golfers that reigned from 1900 to 1914.

Vardon won the British Open six times, and in 1900, he won the U.S. Open as well, sparking some serious interest in the game in America. When he later toured the United States and played matches throughout the country, many who saw him grew eager to play the game. Vardon was the first golfer to support himself as a full-time professional and to live off his earnings from tournaments and exhibition fees.

Using a style of play that was noted for its grace, Vardon popularized the modern overlapping grip that is named for him. He also developed the more modern golf swing that took advantage of the rubber-cored ball. He is remembered fondly for his even temperament, his courage, and his great sportsmanship.

golf

Tom Watson

Tom Watson may be a quiet player, but his golf game shows that still waters run deep. By 1987, after sixteen years on Tour, Watson had won nearly $4.8 million. Only the Golden Bear, Jack Nicklaus, had earned more.

In the early 1970s, Watson lost a number of tournaments, and sportswriters said he choked under pressure. But by the 1977 Masters, which he won by two strokes, Watson had gotten back on top of his game, and he began to amass a string of victories.

Watson's five wins in the British Open include three of the lowest winning totals in the tournament's history. He shot a 268 at Turnberry in 1977, a 271 at Muirfield in 1980, and a 275 at Birkdale in 1983.

Watson won twenty-five Tour events between 1978 and 1987. He has won eight major championships: five British Opens, one U.S. Open, and two Masters. In 1977, Watson was named PGA Player of the Year.

Joyce Wethered

Joyce Wethered, born in England in 1901, was once a student of Harry Vardon. Bobby Jones played with her at St. Andrews in 1930, and afterward marveled that she never missed a shot. "I have no hesitancy in saying that, accounting for the unavoidable handicap of a woman's lesser physical strength, she is the finest golfer I have ever seen," he said.

Tall, slender, and shy, Wethered became an overnight sensation when she won the

1920 English Ladies' Championship at the age of eighteen. She
then went on to win the 1921–1924
Ladies' Championships, and the
British Open in 1922, 1924–1925,
and 1929 as well.

Wethered's swing had a fluid-
ity and grace that impressed all
who watched her play.
Her concentration was
equally remarkable;
some described her
composure as so
strong that it seemed
as if she played in
a trance.

Kathy Whitworth

Kathy Whitworth, a native Texan, was one of a string of Texas players to storm through golf in the mid-twentieth century. In 1957 and 1958, while still in high school, she won the New Mexico Women's Amateur Championship.

Whitworth attended college for one semester, then decided she preferred to play golf. She has won eighty-eight tournaments, more than any player, man or woman. Her career spanned the

1950s to the 1980s.

In 1981, she became the first woman player to reach $1 million in career earnings. Whitworth was the leading money winner eight times, was Player of the Year seven times, won six major championships, and was awarded the Vare Trophy for low scoring seven times.

Whitworth was inducted into the World Golf Hall of Fame in 1982, the Ladies Professional Golf Association Hall of Fame in 1975, and the Women's Sports Foundation Hall of Fame in 1981.

golf

Tiger Woods

When Tiger Woods sank the last putt and won the Master's at Georgia's Augusta National Golf Course in 1997 by an incredible 12-stroke margin, he not only broke the course record, he also became the subject of headline news all around the world. His success has provided the sport of golf with a much-needed shot of adrenaline, creating higher television ratings, increased gallery attendance, and considerably more interest in golf among the young people of America.

Having won three straight U.S. Amateur titles (1994–96) and two U.S. Junior Amateur titles (1992–3), much was expected of Woods once he turned pro—and much was delivered. At twenty-one, he is the youngest golfer ever to win the Masters, and the first African-American (or Asian-American; his mother is Thai) to win any of golf's four major tournaments. Given his age and his success thus far, it is not difficult to envision a bright future for this charismatic young man.

golf

Mickey Wright

In the late 1950s, Mary Kathryn "Mickey" Wright rekindled interest in women's golf, which had fallen into the doldrums after the death of Babe Didrikson Zaharias. A contemporary said, "Mickey got the outside world to take a second look at women golfers and when they looked, they discovered the rest of us."

From 1957 to 1968, Wright earned seventy-nine Tour victories, including fifteen major titles.

She also won the Vare Trophy for low scoring.

In 1961, Wright was the first woman to win three major titles. In 1963, she won thirteen events. Although she is remembered for her many titles, she is also remembered for the way she spurred the press to cover women's golf in a serious way.

golf

Mildred "Babe" Didrikson Zaharias

Mildred Didrikson Zaharias's nickname came from her tomboy baseball days in Texas. Years later, sportswriters named Babe the greatest female athlete of the twentieth century.

She began her career with a bang, as a triple medalist at the 1932 Olympics in Los Angeles. In the tryouts, she competed as a "team" and came out ahead of the second-place team of twenty-two players. She was only allowed to compete in three events; she finished with two golds and a silver.

Before her marriage to professional wrestler George Zaharias, in 1938, Babe played exhibition golf and performed on the vaudeville circuit, tap dancing and playing the harmonica.

In 1946 and 1947, Babe won seventeen consecutive tournaments. She won the U.S. Women's Open in 1948, 1950, and 1954. The last time was while she was battling the cancer that finally claimed her in 1956.

golf

Chapter 7

More
Quips and
Quotes

Real golfers don't cry when they line up their fourth putt.

—*Karen Hurwitz*

The only time you play great golf is when you are doing everything within your power to lose to your boss.

—*Thomas Mulligan*

The rest of the field.

—Roger Maltbie
(when asked what he needed to
shoot to win a tournament)

I'd give up golf if I didn't have so many sweaters.

—Bob Hope

The only way of really finding out a man's true character is to play golf with him. In no other walk of life does the cloven hoof so quickly display itself.

—*P. G. Wodehouse*

— — — — — — — — —

I know I'm getting better at golf because I'm hitting fewer spectators.

—*Gerald Ford*

A professional will tell you the amount of flex you need in the shaft of your club. The more the flex, the more strength you will need to break the thing over your knees.

—*Stephen Baker*

It could be worse; I could be allergic to beer.

—*Greg Norman*
(on being allergic to grass)

golf

Golf is a good walk spoiled.

—*Mark Twain*

Have you ever noticed what golf spells backwards?

—*Al Boliska*

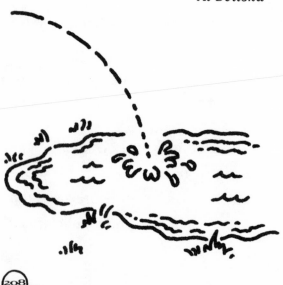

The least thing upset him on the links. He missed short putts because of the uproar of butter-flies in the adjoining meadows.

—*P. G. Wodehouse*

The more I practice, the luckier I get.

—*Gary Player*

golf

In the golf swing, a tiny change can make a huge difference. The natural inclination is to begin to overdo the tiny change that has brought success. So you exaggerate in an effort to improve even more, and soon you are lost and confused again.

—*Harvey Penick*

It's good sportsmanship to not pick up lost golf balls while they are still rolling.

—*Mark Twain*

The inevitable result of any golf lesson is the instant elimination of the one critical unconscious motion that allowed you to compensate for all your errors.

—*Thomas Mulligan*

golf

Most people play a fair game of golf—if you watch them.

—*Joey Adams*

It's a faithless love, but you hit four good shots and you've started your day right.

—*Dinah Shore*

Golfers find it a very trying matter to turn at the waist, more particularly if they have a lot of waist to turn.

—*Harry Vardon*

Well, that lot's full. Let's see if I can park this baby someplace else.

—*Jo Anne Carner*
(on hitting two drives
into a parking lot)

All I could think of was, "Good, I don't have to putt."

—*Mike Blewett*

(on making a hole in one)

If you really want to get better at golf, go back and take it up at a much earlier age.

—*Thomas Mulligan*

I played golf with a priest the other day. . . . He shot par-par-par-par-par. Finally, I said to him, "Father, if you're playing golf like this, you haven't been saving many souls lately."

—*Sam Snead*

You have to play golf in Scotland. What else is there to do there? Wear a skirt?

—*George Low*

Baseball players quit playing and they take up golf. Basketball players quit, take up golf. Football players quit, take up golf. What are we supposed to take up when we quit?

—*George Archer*

We must always be humble in victory and cocky in losing.

—*Chi Chi Rodriguez*

Well, sir, I'd recommend the 4:05 train.

>—*Harry Vardon's caddie*
>*(responding to Vardon's question,*
>*"What should I take here?")*

Anyone who criticizes a golf course is like a person invited to a house for dinner who, on leaving, tells the host that the food was lousy.

>—*Gary Player*

golf

Some of us worship in churches, some in synagogues, some on golf courses.

—*Adlai Stevenson*

Take two weeks off and then quit the game.

—*Jimmy Demaret*
(advice for an unhappy golfer)

Golf is an expensive way of playing marbles.

—*G. K. Chesterton*

The difference between golf and government is that in golf you can't improve your lie.

—*George Deukmejian*

If your opponent is playing several shots in vain attempts to extricate himself from a bunker, do not stand near him and audibly count his strokes. It would be justifiable homicide if he wound up his pitiable exhibition by applying his niblick to your head.

—*Harry Vardon*

It's not whether you win or lose—but whether I win or lose.

—*Sandy Lyle*

My favorite shots are the practice swing and the conceded putt. The rest can never be mastered.

—*Lord Robertson*

The hardest shot is a mashie at ninety yards from the green, where the ball has to be played against an oak tree, bounces back into a sand trap, hits a stone, bounces on the green and then rolls into the cup. That shot is so difficult I have only made it once.

—*Zeppo Marx*

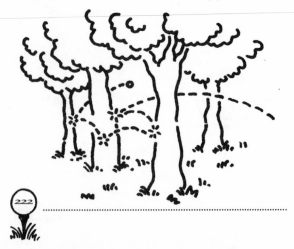

Golf is a better game played
downhill.

—*Jack Nicklaus*

I see things written about the
golf swing that I can't believe
will work except by accident.

—*Harvey Penick*

The person I fear most in the last
two rounds is myself.

—*Tom Watson*

He hits the ball 130 yards and
his jewelry goes 150.

—*Bob Hope (on Sammy Davis Jr.)*

On one hole I'm like Arnold
Palmer, and on the next like Lilli
Palmer.

—*Sean Connery*

Give me my books, my golf
clubs, and leisure, and I would
ask for nothing more.

—*Earl of Balfour*

Golf and sex are the only things
you can enjoy without being
good at them.

—*Jimmy Demaret*

In baseball you hit your home run over the right-field fence, the left-field fence, the center-field fence. Nobody cares. In golf, everything has to go right over second base.

—*Ken Harrelson*

Oh the dirty little pill
Went rolling down the hill
And rolled right into the bunker
From there to the green
I took thirteen
And then by God I sunk her!

—*Traditional*

A day spent in a round of strenu-
ous idleness.

—*William Wordsworth*

Charley hits some good woods—
most of them are trees.

—*Glen Campbell*
(on his friend Charley Pride)

Golf is a game in which the ball lies poorly and the players well.

—Art Rosenbaum

I'll take a 2-shot penalty, but I'll be damned if I'm going to play the ball where it lies.

—Elaine Johnson
(after her tee shot bounced off a tree and landed in her bra)

I'm glad we don't have to play in the shade.

—*Bobby Jones (response to being told it was 105 degrees in the shade)*

I may be the only golfer never to have broken a single putter, if you don't count the one I twisted into a loop and threw into a bush.

—*Thomas Boswell*

golf

When you're having trouble
and topping the ball, it means
the ground is moving on you.

—*Chi Chi Rodriguez*

There are two basic rules which
should never be broken. Be subtle.
And don't, for God's sake, try to
do business with anyone who's
having a bad game.

—*William Davis*

If your adversary is a hole or two down, there is no serious cause for alarm in his complaining of a severely sprained wrist, or an acute pain, resembling lumbago, which checks his swing. Should he happen to win the next hole, these symptoms will in all probability become less troublesome.

—*Horace Hutchinson*

Chapter 8

By the
Numbers

British Open

British Open Champions

1980 Tom Watson

1981 Bill Rogers

1982 Tom Watson

1983 Tom Watson

1984 Seve Ballesteros

1985 Sandy Lyle

1986 Greg Norman

1987 Nick Faldo

1988 Seve Ballesteros

1989 Mark Calcavecchia

1990 Nick Faldo

1991 Ian Baker-Finch

1992 Nick Faldo

1993 Greg Norman

1994 Nick Price

1995 John Daly

1996 Tom Lehman

1997 Justin Leonard

All-Time British Open Records
Most wins: Harry Vardon won six
times (1896, 1898–1899, 1903,
1911, 1914).

Most consecutive wins: Tom Morris Jr. won four times (1868–1870, 1872). There was no British Open in 1871.

Lowest eighteen-hole total: Seven players have had 63s: Mark Hayes (1977), Isao Aoki (1980), Greg Norman (1986), Paul Broadhurst (1990), Jodie Mudd (1991), Nick Faldo (1993), and Payne Stewart (1993).

Lowest seventy-two-hole total: 267, Greg Norman's score in 1993.

Oldest champion: Tom Morris Sr. won in 1867 when he was forty-six years, ninety-nine days. Youngest champion: Tom Morris Jr. won in 1868 when he was seventeen years, 249 days.

The Masters

Masters Champions

1980 Seve Ballesteros

1981 Tom Watson

1982 Craig Stadler

1983 Seve Ballesteros

1984 Ben Crenshaw

1985 Bernhard Langer

1986 Jack Nicklaus

1987 Larry Mize

1988 Sandy Lyle

1989 Nick Faldo

1990 Nick Faldo

1991 Ian Woosnam

1992 Fred Couples

1993 Bernhard Langer

1994 José Maria Olazabal

1995 Ben Crenshaw

1996 Nick Faldo

1997 Tiger Woods

1998 Mark O'Meara

All-Time Masters Records
Most wins: Jack Nicklaus had six wins (1963, 1965–1966, 1972, 1975, 1986).

golf

Most consecutive wins: Only two players, Jack Nicklaus (1965–1966) and Nick Faldo (1989–1990), have won two Masters in a row.

Lowest eighteen-hole total: Both Nick Price (1986) and Greg Norman (1996) had record eighteen-hole totals of 63.

Lowest seventy-two-hole total: Tiger Woods won in 1997 with a 270.

Oldest champion: Jack Nicklaus, who won in 1986 at the age of forty-six years, eighty-one days.

Youngest champion: Tiger Woods, who was twenty-one years, 104 days old when he won in 1997.

U.S. Open

U.S. Open Champions

1980 Jack Nicklaus

1981 David Graham

1982 Tom Watson

1983 Larry Nelson

1984 Fuzzy Zoeller

1985 Andy North

1986 Raymond Floyd

1987 Scott Simpson

1988 Curtis Strange

1989 Curtis Strange

1990 Hale Irwin

1991 Payne Stewart

1992 Tom Kite

1993 Lee Janzen

1994 Ernie Els

1995 Corey Pavin

1996 Steve Jones

1997 Ernie Els

All-Time U.S. Open Records
Most wins: Four players have won this title four times each: Willie Anderson (1901, 1903–1905), Bobby Jones (1923, 1926,

1929–1930), Ben Hogan (1948, 1950–1951, 1953), and Jack Nicklaus (1962, 1967, 1972, 1980).

Most consecutive wins: Willie Anderson won three times (1903–1905).

Lowest eighteen-hole total: Three players scored 63: Johnny Miller in 1973; Jack Nicklaus and Tom Weiskopf in 1980.

Lowest seventy-two-hole total: Two players had 272: Jack Nicklaus in 1980 and Lee Janzen in 1993.

Oldest champion: Hale Irwin, who won in 1990 at the age of forty-five years, fifteen days.

Youngest champion: John J. McDermott, who was nineteen years, 317 days old when he won in 1911.

golf

PGA
Championship

PGA Champions

1980 Jack Nicklaus

1981 Larry Nelson

1982 Raymond Floyd

1983 Hal Sutton

1984 Lee Trevino

1985 Hubert Green

1986 Bob Tway

1987 Larry Nelson

1988 Jeff Sluman

1989 Payne Stewart

1990 Wayne Grady

1991 John Daly

1992 Nick Price

1993 Paul Azinger

1994 Ernie Els

1995 Steve Elkington

1996 Mark Brooks

1997 Davis Love III

All-Time PGA Championship Records
Most wins: Both Walter Hagen
(1921, 1924–1927) and Jack

Nicklaus (1963, 1971, 1973, 1975, 1980) have won this title five times.

Most consecutive wins: Walter Hagen, with four wins (1924–1927).

Lowest eighteen-hole total: Six players have had low scores of 63: Bruce Crampton (1975), Ray Floyd (1982), Gary Player (1984), Vijay Singh (1993), Michael Bradley (1995), and Brad Faxon (1995).

By the Numbers

Lowest seventy-two-hole total: Two players have had scores of 267: Steve Elkington (1995) and Colin Montgomerie (1995).

Oldest champion: Julius Boros, who was forty-eight years, 140 days when he won in 1968.

Youngest champion: Gene Sarazen, who was twenty years, 173 days when he won in 1922.

golf

The Grand Slam

Most Major Titles

Jack Nicklaus has won eighteen majors (three British Opens, four U.S. Opens, five PGA Championships, and six Masters), more than any other golfer. Walter Hagen comes next with eleven majors (four British Opens, two U.S. Opens, and five PGA Championships).

Only Bobby Jones has won all four majors in one year to win the Grand Slam. Ben Hogan,

Jack Nicklaus, Gary Player, and Gene Sarazen have each won all four majors at one point or another, but not in the same year.

golf

PGA All-Time Leaders

All-Time Career Wins

81 Sam Snead

70 Jack Nicklaus

63 Ben Hogan

60 Arnold Palmer

52 Byron Nelson

51 Billy Casper

40 Walter Hagen

40 Cary Middlecoff

Women's U.S. Open

Women's U.S. Open Champions

1980 Amy Alcott

1981 Pat Bradley

1982 Janet Anderson

1983 Jan Stephenson

1984 Hollis Stacy

1985 Kathy Baker

1986 Jane Geddes

1987 Laura Davies

1988 Liselotte Neumann

golf

1989 Betsy King

1990 Betsy King

1991 Meg Mallon

1992 Patty Sheehan

1993 Laurie Merten

1994 Patty Sheehan

1995 Annika Sorenstam

1996 Annika Sorenstam

1997 Alison Nicolas

All-Time Women's U.S. Open Records
Most wins: Betsy Rawls (1951,
1953, 1957, 1960) and Mickey

Wright (1958–1959, 1961, 1964) have each won it four times.

Most consecutive wins: Six players have won two in a row: Mickey Wright (1958–1959), Donna Caponi (1969–1970), Susie Berning (1972–1973), Hollis Stacy (1977–1978), Betsy King (1989–1990), Annika Sorenstam (1995–1996).

Lowest eighteen-hole total: Helen Alfredsson had a 63 in 1994.

Lowest seventy-two-hole total:
Liselotte Neumann had a 277 in
1988.

Oldest champion: Fay Croker won
in 1955 when she was forty
years, 335 days.

Youngest champion: Catherine
Lacoste won in 1967 when she
was twenty-two years, five days.

LPGA Tour Records

Most Career Wins

88 Kathy Whitworth

82 Mickey Wright

57 Patty Berg

55 Betsy Rawls

50 Louise Suggs

48 Nancy Lopez

42 Jo Anne Carner

42 Sandra Haynie

38 Carol Mann

golf

All-Time LPGA Records

Most wins (season): Mickey
Wright, with thirteen in 1963.

Most consecutive wins: Both
Mickey Wright (1962–1963) and
Kathy Whitworth (1969) have
four consecutive wins.

Widest margin of victory: Louise Suggs won the U.S. Open in 1949 by fourteen strokes, as did Cindy Mackey in the MasterCard International in 1986.

golf

Chapter 9

A Golfer's Guide to the Internet

Comprehensive Sites

Golf Web

http://www.golfweb.com

One of the premier spots on the Web to learn about what's going on in the world of golf. Using its links to an estimated 60,000 pages, you can find all the basics about golf on Golf Web. You can also connect to the CBS SportsLine, scan a weekly poll on various golfing issues, and learn

what's new in golfing software.
There's even a link to OnCourse,
a searchable database with information on more than 20,000 golf
courses in the United States.

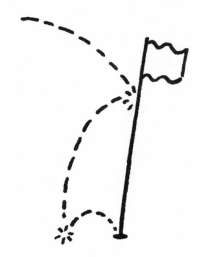

golf

iGOLF

http://www.igolf.com

Magnificent golfers' domain with news and feature stories, plenty of instructional information, and a searchable directory via which you can find just what you're looking for. Win prizes in the iGOLF Challenge, learn all about new equipment, or join the iGOLF player's club and receive a 10 percent discount in the pro shop.

The USGA:
United States Golf Association
http://www.usga.org

The USGA home page offers an abundance of information about the rules of golf. There's also the Greens Section, dedicated to the construction and maintenance of greens. Also learn about the handicap system, get the latest stats on championships, and read all the latest news in the world of golf.

golf

*Women's Golf at the
Mining Company*

http://womensgolf.miningco.
com/mbody.htm

Hosted by Bill D'Zurilla, this Mining Company site includes information specific to women's golf. There's a women's golf chat room, a bookstore, and a Women's Golf Scholarship Guide that's captioned, "You can get a golf scholarship if you can break 100!"

Yahoo! Sports:
Men's Professional Golf

http://golf.yahoo.com/pga

Want to see the leaderboard for
the hottest tournament in
progress? Planning a vacation and
want to know about golf courses
where you're going? You'll find
those things along with links to
women's and
senior's golf at
this Yahoo!-
sponsored site.

golf

Golf Links

Golf Link

http://www.golflink.
net/homepages/links/hotlist.htm

The links on this page are conveniently categorized into folders, with links to U.S. and international golf sites. You can find news and information, services, merchandise, material on events and celebrities, and more. A nice set of links.

Sanford Associates

http://www.sanford-golf.
com/sa-link.html

More links than you thought
existed, brought to you by
Sanford Associates, a landscape
and golf architectural firm in
Jupiter, Florida. Find links to
FAQs (frequently asked questions)
about golf; golf in the UK,
Europe, and Asia; several different golf magazines; and a whole
lot more. Plan to spend a lot of
time here. Following all these
links could take days.

golf

Golf-Related Merchandise

Golf Ball Warehouse

http://www.myballs.com

How about some free golf balls, or some low golf ball prices? The Golf Ball Warehouse touts itself as the "largest supplier of new and used golf balls on the Web." Learn some tips, visit the reading room, and amaze yourself with some golf ball trivia. You can also test your knowledge or laugh at a few jokes.

Seabury's

http://www.clever.net/
wwwmall/seaburys

Women's golf togs, jewelry and accessories, shoes, and more can be found at this site. This is also a good place to select a special gift for that golfing guy in your life. You can view the photo of your gift online and order toll-free by phone.

golf

Golf Shoes Plus

http://www.golfshoesplus.
com/index.htm

Hailed as "one of the largest sports shoe sites on the Internet," men's and women's styles from Footjoy, Florsheim, Etonic, and other big-name golf shoe manufacturers are offered here. Photos of the shoes will help with your selection, and you can order over the phone via an 800 number or fax. You can also order online through a secure connection.

Golf Travel

Golf Travel Web Ireland

http://www.golfingireland.
com/home.shtml

Find hotels and resorts, golf
courses, and even sample
itineraries for spending a golfing
holiday in Ireland.

golf

Hawaii Golf Courses

http://www2.hawaii.edu/
golfstuff/golf_courses.html

Planning on going to Hawaii?
This site lists all the golf courses
available on each island and their
rates. Some of the courses are
mapped.

MAXimum Golf Planner

http://www.aesir.com/MAXimum/
GolfPlanner/Welcome.htm

Thinking of taking a golf vacation at Hilton Head Island, South Carolina? This site will allow you to locate all the courses on the island or it will pick one at random for you and describe it in detail. You'll be able to see the course stats and scorecards for some of the courses.

golf

Just for Fun

Classic Club Auction

http://www.oneputt.com/classic

In the market for a hickory-shafted Otey Christman model 16HBW? You can see photos and bid for collectable clubs at this page on the A Quality Golf Company site. Winning bidders must be completely satisfied with their purchase or the company guarantees that their money will be "cheerfully refunded."

St. Duffer

http://www.st-duffer
.com/duffer.html

Did you know there was a patron
saint for golf? James Duffer
achieved sainthood one day after
playing seventeen perfect holes of
golf, then choking on the eighteenth. Since then, golfers all
over the world have destroyed
clubs in hopes that St. Duffer
will chaperon their unruly balls
to the hole. Learn all about St.
Duffer's miracles and enjoy a
chuckle.

·······································➤ **golf**

Usenet

Usenet is a group of bulletin board–type discussion groups that are loosely based upon a theme. Golf has a number of newsgroups to amuse you. Try one or all of these:

alt.golfing-with-orson-beene

fj.rec.sports.golf

pdaxs.sports.golf

pdx.golf

rec.sport.golf

Utilities

....

Course Handicap Calculator

http://pas1.erols.com/rivercup

/handicap.html-ssi

You know what your personal handicap is . . . but what about a specific course handicap? You'll find the calculator here plus much more.

....➤ golf

Shawguides: Golf Schools

http://www.shawguides.
com/cgi-bin/rbox/sg.pl?s=1

Looking for a school where you can learn to play golf? Have no fear, Shawguides is here. Just choose your preferences from a handy drop-down index and click "go." You'll be provided a list of golf schools in any area or state you specify. Links to some of the schools' Web sites and e-mail addresses are available there too.

Van's Repair Center

http://www.vansgolf.com/

johnnytee.html

Have a favorite or lucky club that you need repaired? Have you ever wanted a club made specifically for you? Johnny T. can help. Check out the center and see what's on special.

golf

Chapter 10

Sure-Shot

Tips

The First Tee

We've all experienced nerves on the first tee, especially if other golfers are waiting to tee off. If you have a pre-shot routine, using it can be particularly helpful in calming the jitters. You don't need to spend a lot of time over this first shot—and you don't need to kill the ball. Think of the first shot as just another practice swing. Don't be surprised if your first drive turns out to be the best of the day.

Keep It Moving

A round of golf should take no more than four hours. This is important because the rhythm of the game and the ability to stay focused are disrupted by delays in play. Always think about your next shot while walking or riding to your ball. If you're uncertain about the distance of the shot, take two clubs to the ball. Take *one* practice swing, if that. Then hit the ball and move along.

golf

Pre-Shot Routine

Having a pre-shot routine is an effective way of reducing tension while playing. Once you've determined which club to use, stand behind the ball and visualize the shot (the flight of the ball). Then address the ball, aiming the club at the intermediate target. Turn your head (without lifting it) to take a last look at the target, take a deep breath, and let it rip.

286

Grip Pressure

Grip pressure will go a long way in determining how well you swing the club. Gripping the club too firmly will decrease your club head speed. What's too firmly? Your initial pressure should be just enough to hold onto the club if someone were to pull on it. The majority of the pressure should come from the last three fingers of the left hand and the two middle fingers of the right. By the way, having a worn grip may cause you to grip the club too firmly.

golf

Balance

Good balance results in a seemingly effortless swing. Watch the pros: On their backswing, their right foot never rolls to the right but remains flat. And on the follow-through, their weight is directly above the left foot. To practice balance, hit half-shots with a sand or pitching wedge. On the takeaway (backswing), don't take your left arm beyond a position parallel with the ground. On the follow-through, stop with your right arm parallel to the ground.

The Takeaway

A proper takeaway, or backswing, is essential in developing a consistent swing. Begin the swing by keeping the club low and the triangle formed by your arms and shoulders intact until the club is parallel to the ground. If you stopped at this point, your right hand would be in position to shake hands with someone standing to your right and the head of the club would be pointing up.

golf

Loading Up

"Loading up" is one of the major ways power is generated in a golf swing. Look at a pro. The pro's shoulders will turn ninety degrees, but his or her hips turn only about half that amount. This winds up the body like a coiled spring, referred to as "loading up." Getting to this position requires flexibility and practice. Don't let your hips rotate too far. Work on keeping your right knee in a flexed position as you take the club back to limit your hip turn.

Practice the Short Game

Most practice time is spent working on the full swing. However,
the fastest way to lower your
score is by improving your short
game. Find a practice facility
with a putting green, sand trap,
and a place to practice chips and
pitch shots—
or else, go to
a nearby park
or school play-
ground—and
practice!

golf

Chipping

When chipping around the green, try using the same grip as when you putt. The stroke also will resemble your putting stroke. Keep the majority of your weight on your left foot. Your hands should stay relaxed for better feel. Distance is controlled by the length of the stroke. As in a putt, it is important to accelerate the club through the ball, being sure not to allow your left wrist to break.

Putting Basics

Many times it seems that putting is really a separate game from golf. Even if you are one of the fortunate few who is a natural at putting, all of us can improve if we remember a few simple rules. Good putters usually share three traits. First, they have their eyes directly over the ball or just slightly inside. Second, good putters move their arms and shoulders as one unit. Finally, good putters accelerate the club through the ball.

golf

Putting Maxims

When you're putting, don't lift your head until you hear the ball clink in the cup (or you're sure it hasn't). When you're putting downhill, hold the putter more loosely.

First Putting Drill

To find out if your eyes are over the ball, take a putting stance with a ball placed on the ground. Then take another ball in your hand, hold it up between your eyes, and drop it to see where it lands. If it drops onto the ball already on the ground, your eyes are directly over the ball.

Second Putting Drill

To get the feeling that your arms and shoulders are a unit, put your arms through a coat hanger (with the flat side toward your body). The hanger should be just above your elbows. Hit some putts and notice how your arms and shoulders work together.

Third Putting Drill

To practice accelerating through the ball, place a ball about a foot from the hole and push the ball into the hole with the putter. Do this ten times and then move the ball three feet from the hole. Now take the putter back a few inches and hit the ball. After hitting the ball, "chase the ball" with the putter, attempting to hit it again as it rolls toward the hole.

Putting Speed

For best results, develop a routine before each putt and stick to it. Remember that proper speed is the most important element of a putt. If you hit the ball at the proper speed, it will take the break you expect and get to the hole. Don't make your putting stroke too long—keep the stroke short enough so that you have to accelerate through the ball.

Sand Play

No shot seems to cause more tension for the average golfer than the sand shot. In order to avoid short, quick stabs at the sand, practice visualizing the shot and think about where you want the ball to land. Grip the club lightly, make sure you take a slow, full backswing, then accelerate the club through the sand. Control the distance of the shot with the length of your follow-through. The longer the shot, the longer the follow-through.

golf

Quick Fix

One common cause of trouble in golf is lining up too far to the right of the target. To check whether your shoulders are pointing toward the target, set up to the shot, and then take the club in your right hand and put it across your chest at shoulder height. The club should be pointing along the line you want to start the ball or just slightly to the left.

Another Quick Fix

To check to see if your ball position is correct, address the ball with both feet together. Now move each foot an equal distance apart; this will put the ball in the proper position. For some golfers, this check is a part of their pre-shot routine.

golf

High Percentage Shots

It can be tempting to try to hit a difficult shot, even though there may be little chance of success. You may have the urge to play the big hook from behind the tree to the green, or to hit a fairway wood over a tree and make it home. The odds are against you, especially if you haven't practiced trouble shots at the range. You'd be surprised how well you'll do by playing safe instead and getting the ball back into play.

Hit Down with Your Irons

In order to get your iron shots up in the air with consistency, be sure to hit down on the ball. A good indication that you are hitting down is that you take a divot on your iron shots. At address, be sure that your hands are even with or slightly ahead of the ball. This will help promote a descending blow.

golf

Splash the Sand

A sand shot is unique because you don't hit the ball first. Think of the sand as water, and proceed as if you're going to splash the water with the bottom of the club. Take an open stance with the club face pointing at the target. Allow the club to swing back along your shoulder line. Then concentrate on splashing the sand with the bottom of the club a few inches behind the ball. Be sure to keep the club moving through the sand to a full follow-through.

Playing in the Wind

Playing when the wind is in your face may cause you to grip the club too tightly. This creates tension in your arms, resulting in a swing that's too hard. At address, see how lightly you can grip the club and how smoothly you can take it back. Concentrate on making a full swing while staying in balance. The key is to hit the ball as solidly as you can and realize that the ball just isn't going to fly as far.

Swing Your Arms

Sam Snead once said he never saw a bad practice swing. When someone is making a practice swing, there is no tension; the person just swings his arms and lets his body move naturally. Here's a good drill to practice to learn to swing your arms: Take a 5-iron, take a relaxed grip, and place your feet *together*. Now, just swing your arms and hit shots. If you're losing your balance, you're swinging too hard.

Tempo Tip

Good tempo in a golf swing is critical. If you think you're having trouble with your tempo, try this: Using a 5-iron, address the ball as you normally would. Then take the club and put it about ten to twelve inches in front of the ball. Start your swing from this position. You'll find that having to take the club back that extra distance will slow up your swing.

golf

Another Tempo Tip

If you're on the course and feel that your tempo is off, take your driver and hold it just below the head of the club (upside down). Now make some practice swings. Not having the weight of the club head will slow your swing down and improve your tempo.

Enjoy Yourself

Don't forget that golf is only a game. Enjoy yourself! Be sure that you set reasonable expectations. Many golfers expect more than they are capable of achieving. Of course, practice is important. As Gary Player said, "The more I play, the luckier I get." If you set reasonable expectations, practice as much as you can, and take lessons from a pro you respect, your game should improve—and most important, you should enjoy yourself.

golf

Chapter 11

Tournaments

The Alfred Dunhill Cup

Since 1985, the St. Andrews Golf Links Old Course has hosted an October tournament, the Alfred Dunhill Cup, which sports teams from around the world. Sixteen nations compete, each represented by a three-man team. The teams compete man-to-man, in medal play format. The man in each pairing with the lowest eighteen-hole score is the winner.

Tournament play starts with four-team groupings, which play

round robins for three days. The Dunhill tests staying power as well as skill, the champion having to win two matches in one day.

The championship has been rumored to be seeking a new home. October weather in St. Andrews has caused even the tournament's world-class golfers to cringe. However, it appears that the Old Course will be the tournament site at least until the millennium.

golf

The British Open Championship

The British Open, begun in 1860, was the first championship open to golf professionals. Since 1919, both it and the British Amateur Championship have been managed by the Royal and Ancient Golf Club of St. Andrews. How steeped in British tradition can you get?

Today this championship may be conducted at any one of eight courses in Scotland and England, all of them named to delight the Anglophile. Royal

Lytham and St. Anne's Golf Club, the Royal Liverpool Golf Club, St. Andrews, and Muirfield lead the list. The British is British from head to toe.

Although the tournament is unmistakably British, Americans have had considerable success here. Since Walter Hagen won in 1922, the title has gone to an American thirty times.

In 1969, when the British Open had not been won by a Briton for eighteen years, Tony Jacklin returned the championship to its namesake country.

The Nabisco Dinah Shore Championship

A little over a quarter century ago, talk show hostess Dinah Shore sponsored a golf tournament that has an audience substantially larger than her show ever had. Mission Hills Country Club in Rancho Mirage, California, is the site of this first ladies' major event.

Like the men's Masters, this prestigious tournament is held every year at the same golf course and is a local tradition, sweeping San Diego into a week of red-teed golf frenzy. The event earned official major championship status in 1983, and has become a major draw for top women golfers and entertainers.

Politics has also made its way into this tournament. Important female politicians join the clouds of showbiz celebrities at parties, shows, and rallies. Dinah Shore's power as a woman of achievement is commemorated here in the demonstrated ability of women, both as golfers and as participants in society.

Doral-Ryder Open

The Blue Course at the Doral
Country Club and Spa in Miami
was designed in 1961 and one
short year later, the first Doral-
Ryder Open was sponsored by
developer Alfred Kaskel.

The Blue Course is known as
"The Blue Monster" because of
its eight expansive water hazards
that affect twelve holes. Although
no golfers have been lost to
gators or other denizens of the
converted swampland, many have

"drowned" in the multiple water hazards of this challenging course.

Although the Doral sports several repeat winners, only one golfer, Raymond Floyd, has been able to successfully defend a championship. Certainly the 107 sand bunkers and the 435-yard final hole, mostly water and sand, have a lot to do with the one-year reign of most champions.

The 1997 winner's purse of $324,000 dwarfs the first purse of $50,000 offered in 1962—and in 1962, the Doral was the richest golf tournament in America.

golf

The Masters

Since it began in 1934, the Masters at Augusta National Golf Club has been steeped in legend and magic. The course is marked by the natural glory of spring. Its blaze of flowers has named the holes of the course, which include Yellow Jasmine, Carolina Cherry, Flowering Peach, and Tea Olive.

In 1997, Tiger Woods set several records at the Masters. He was the first minority golfer to win the tournament, the youngest Masters champion ever (he was only twenty-one)—and he had the lowest score ever for the tournament. He had been a professional golfer for only seven and a half months before winning his green jacket.

At the other end of the spectrum, Doug Ford set a Masters record in 1997 by playing in his forty-fifth Masters. Since the Masters invites all living ex-champions to each competition, Tiger Woods, given moderate longevity, may someday break Ford's record.

The AT&T Pebble Beach National Pro-Am

The Pebble Beach Golf Links provide one of the most challenging sequences on the professional golf tour. Located on California's Seventeen-Mile Drive between Monterey and Carmel, the course overlooks the Pacific Ocean, and the competitors must pay attention to challenges of both the holes and the ocean breezes.

Competitors in this tournament play preliminary rounds on

three different courses—the 6,799-yard Pebble Beach Golf Links, the 6,859-yard Spyglass Hill Country Club, and the 6,861-yard Poppy Hills Golf Club. The final round, played on the fourth day of the tournament, is played at the namesake Pebble Beach Golf Links.

Observant early-morning spectators at the Pro-Am might see the deer that frequent the golf links, or the sea otters, seals, and cormorants that challenge the surf just across the road.

PGA Championship

It's as demanding as the U.S. Open and it's the last tournament of the season. It's hot, the players are tired, and the format is stroke play, not match play, as it used to be. The courses are chosen for their long roughs beside the greens and along the fairways. It's Darwinian, for sure.

This championship has become less attractive to European golfers over the past few decades, especially since qualification is based on performances in the U.S. Tour.

The tournament has been around since 1916, with Jack Nicklaus pretty much duplicating his U.S. Open record list. He has played in the PGA Championship thirty-four times, and won it five times. This championship remains the one major that Arnold Palmer never won.

The Ryder Cup

In 1926, a gentleman's match was played between representatives of the American and British Golfers' Associations. The British won by a wide margin. A wealthy British seed merchant, Samuel A. Ryder, offered a solid gold trophy to be awarded each year to the winner of a similar match.

The match has since been expanded to include European golfers as well. Participants in the Ryder Cup are not playing for prize money. They are given generous expenses, but the profits from the event go to the professional associations that host it.

The three-day tournament involves a total of 28 points. Matches include two-ball and four-ball two-man team golf (foursomes) and singles competitions. A win gives the team 1 point; a halved match, a half-point. The first team to amass 14 points wins the Ryder Cup.

golf

The GTE Classic

Since 1980, the PGA Senior Tour has provided competition and career extension for professional golfers age fifty and over. The annual GTE Classic, held at TPC in Tampa Bay, Florida, combines spirited competition with a strong sense of public service. In 1997, Florida charities received over $400,000 from this tournament.

The GTE Classic is filled with golf legends. The indefatigable Bob Charles has never missed a Classic and is the event's only double winner. And in 1998, the MasterCard Champions—players over sixty—will engage in a tournament within a tournament, a thirty-six-hole, two-day event, with a winner's purse of $18,000.

Talk about competitive! No player has ever won a GTE Classic without posting at least one round in the 70s. In 1996, none of the players broke par, due in large part to the weather.

The Skins Game

The term "skins" was coined at the origin of golf, St. Andrews in Scotland. The seaside golf course once attracted incoming traders who would anchor offshore and then play their way into town over the eleven holes of the Old Course. As they played, they would bet on the holes in their stock-in-trade—animal pelts.

Today, this championship is no longer a betting affair between the golfers, although it is a fierce competition in which big money is won or lost. The first six holes are worth $20,000 each; the middle six, $30,000 each; and the final six, $40,000 each. Four carefully selected competitors go for the bucks in this exciting play-off.

Unlike other "big name" golf events, this tournament does not lead to a championship. It only leads to money for the winners of the individual holes. The hole-at-a-time payoff process creates a wide-open competition, which has earned this tournament a huge following among spectators.

The U.S. Women's Open Championship

The Women's Professional Golfers Association ran the first U.S. Women's Open in 1946. When that organization vanished, the Ladies Professional Golf Association took its place as the organizer of the event.

In 1953, the USGA became the tournament's sponsor, at the request of the LPGA. That year, the championship was held at the Country Club of Rochester in New

York, with prize money of $75,000.

1965 was a watershed year for the tournament, as its final round was broadcast nationwide. Both the tournament and women's professional golf were ready to explode onto the sports scene. In 1995, the purse for the Women's Open broke the million-dollar mark.

This tournament is so competitive that no woman has won three consecutive championships, although both Betsy Rawls and Mickey Wright have won it a total of four times each.

The Hawaiian Open

The Uniden/United Airlines Hawaiian Open is the most widely visible sports event in Hawaii or the Pacific. In 1998, 220 million TV households will have access to the match.

The 6,975-yard, par-72 Waialae Country Club in Honolulu hosts the event. The club has instituted a rule that may surprise many: Its members and guests are required to wear spikeless shoes.

The Open is a true community event, and its organizers take care to make it accessible to as many people as possible. Daily admission tickets have stayed the same price ($8 and $10) for nine years now, barely more than admission to a movie.

The 1998 winner's prize of $234,000 is rich—and it may be supplemented by a win in the six-hole Shootout. A dozen top pro golfers compete, with the two laggards eliminated after each hole until only two remain to compete for the top prize of $5,500.

The U.S. Open

The U.S. Open is perhaps the world's most prestigious golf tournament. Its location varies from year to year. Only the most exacting, demanding, and carefully maintained of the United States' golf courses may host this grandfather of American golf tourneys.

The USGA is often criticized for its choice of demanding courses that draw bogeys and make par a blessing and birdies a rarity. But the golfers who win the right to compete and the crowds who cheer their efforts believe that the most prestigious of tournaments demands the most challenging of courses.

The first U.S. Open was held in 1895 and was an add-on to an amateur event that featured a golfer who substituted a pool cue for a putter. The field of eleven professionals competed for a purse of $150.

golf

The du Maurier Classic

The du Maurier Classic is the only stop on the LPGA Tour to be played north of the border and is also the yearly end of the LPGA majors. As do other nations with important tournaments, Canada graciously welcomes golfers from around the world but craves a champion from its own heritage.

Only Jocelyn Bourassa, winner of the first du Maurier in 1973, has gained victory for Canada.

The tournament faces a

threat to its survival, despite having progressed from a $50,000 purse in 1973 to $1.2 million in 1997 (1997 winner's share: $180,000). The sponsorship of the tournament is under attack. Canadian legislation aimed at reducing tobacco's publicity endangers the du Maurier name on this and other Canadian cultural and sporting events.

golf

The McDonald's LPGA Championship

This tournament, the second oldest in LPGA history, was first held in 1955. It has grown into one of the four women's majors and one of the most important charity fund-raisers in the world

The McDonald's is one of the two richest tournaments on the LPGA Tour. In 1997, the tournament donated $1,800,000—over half a million more than that year's tournament purse—to the

Ronald McDonald House Charities, which provides grants to not-for-profit children's organizations around the world. Over its forty-one years, the tournament has raised $25,500,000 for Ronald McDonald House Charities.

This springtime tournament features some of the top names in golf and some of the toughest golf competition in the world. The forty-one past winners of the McDonald's include nineteen members of the LPGA Hall of Fame.

golf

Chapter 12

Gifts for

Golfers

Golf towels

Books relating to golf

Golf notecards

Computer game with golf theme

Golf jacket

Subscription to a golf magazine

Membership in USGA

Autographed golf card

Gifts for Golfers

Instructional golf video

Antique golf equipment such as
old putters, mashies, etc.

Golfing calendars

Golf lessons

Personalized golf tees

Tickets to a golf tournament

Head covers for woods

golf

Tripod tees to use on
hard ground

Plastic tubes to protect
shafts of clubs

Golf gloves

Visor or cap

Trolley for pulling golf bags

Golf balls

Gifts for Golfers

Ball marker

Rain pants and jacket

Golf mug

Indoor practice
equipment for putting

Putter

golf

Chapter 13

Did You

Know?

The first recorded mention of golf clubs in the United States occurred in 1729, when golf "sticks" were listed in an account of the estate of William Burnet, governor of New York and Massachusetts.

In 1912, Harry Dearth boasted that he could play a match while wearing a suit of armor—which he then proceeded to do.

President Dwight D. Eisenhower loved golf passionately, but like most players, he often struggled with his game. During the 1956 election campaign, bumper stickers could be seen with the message: "Ben Hogan for President. If We're Going To Have a Golfer in the White House, Make Him a Good One."

Only in the 1930s did golf club manufacturers start building matched sets of clubs. The steel shaft made this possible; prior to this time, wooden-shafted clubs (mostly made of hickory) were sold individually.

George Grant invented the golf tee in 1899, for which he was granted patent number 638,920. Before tees were used, golfers would build a small pile of dirt or sand for the golf ball to sit on.

The longest hole in one ever recorded was hit by Robert Mitera in Omaha, Nebraska. Playing on the Miracle Hill golf course in 1965, Mitera drove 447 yards off the tenth tee, right into the cup. He was aided by a downhill slope and a favorable breeze.

The golf color barrier was not broken until 1975, when the Masters Tournament invited black competitor Lee Elder to play.

Par, the number of strokes that it should take a superior golfer to complete a particular hole with no mistakes, is largely based on the length of the hole (although the difficulty caused by aspects of the terrain is sometimes taken into account as well). The guidelines used by USGA for par on distance (in yards) alone are as follows:

Par	Men	Women
3	up to 250	up to 210
4	251–470	211–400
5	over 470	401–575

One of the reasons why golf is such a difficult and frustrating game is that you have at least three minutes to think about what you're going to do before each shot. In other sports, such as basketball, football, or tennis, you simply react—the ball comes at you, and you respond—which is altogether an easier task.

Several decades ago, when the Tournament of Champions was played in Las Vegas, the prize money was issued in silver dollars.

 You should always keep track of your pencil! Some say it will bring bad luck if you leave it in the clubhouse and have to borrow one from your partner.

The USGA decrees that golfers must play with balls no smaller than 1.68 inches in diameter, but they do not impose a limit on how big the balls can be. Technically, you can play with as big a ball as you want—but don't expect a big one to go farther than a small one.

Some players believe that it is bad luck to stumble on the steps leading from the fourth tee.

 At one point during the 1920 British Open, George Duncan was thirteen strokes behind the leader, but he still went on to win the tournament.

Tom Morris Sr. won the British Open in 1862 by an astounding thirteen strokes.

When playing on a goodwill tour in South America, Sam Snead became entangled with an ostrich and ended up with the ostrich's beak clamped to his hand.

A gopher in Winnipeg with a liking for taking golf balls from a nearby course was discovered to have stashed over 250 balls in its nest.

On August 19, 1962, twenty-four-year-old Homero Blancas broke the record of 59 for tournament golf with a score of 55 in the Premier Invitational at Premier Golf Course, Longview, Texas. The previous record had been jointly held by Sam Snead and Earl Fry.

Doug Sanders lost the 1970 Open by missing a three-foot putt on the last green at St. Andrews.

When Nick Faldo played in the Ryder Cup two decades ago, he was the youngest player to ever do so. He still holds that record today.

golf

Few sports records stand the test of time, but Edward Bliss's 445-yard shot stood in first place for more than fifty years. The fifty-year-old Bliss clubbed the historic shot in 1913 at Old Course at Herne Bay, Kent, England. The quarter-mile-plus trip included the bouncing and rolling of the ball.

 England's Ladies Golf Union organized the first women's golf championship on a full course in 1893—in spite of the Victorian male perception that "constitutionally and physically, women are unfitted for golf."

In 1954, Laddie Lukas shot a round of golf in eighty-seven strokes at the Sandy Lodge Golf Course in England—a decent accomplishment under normal circumstances, but on this occasion Lukas was wearing a blindfold.

Astronaut Alan B. Shepard hit a golf ball 200 yards on the Moon on February 6, 1971.

🏐 Harry Vardon missed a six-inch putt while playing in the 1913 U.S. Open, necessitating a three-way play-off, which he lost.

🏐 The early gutta-percha balls had a tendency to split into pieces. An early rule for their play allowed the owner of a split ball to place another ball where the largest portion of the split ball lay.

P. G. Wodehouse, English writer and humorist, wrote the following dedication in his book *Golf Without Tears:* "To the immortal memory of John Henrie and Pat Rogie who at Edinburgh, in the year A.D. 1593, were imprisoned for 'Playing of the gowf on the links of Leith every sabbath at the time of the sermonses.'"

Did You Know?

 While playing on a course in North Carolina in 1939, R. R. Smiley hit a hole in one from the thirteenth tee. The only problem was that the hole the ball rolled into was the eleventh, not the thirteenth.

golf

Chapter 14

Quiz

Yourself

Q What is a mashie?

A A mashie is the name given to the early golf club that was the equivalent of a 5-iron.

Q Why is a game of golf referred to as a "round of golf"?

A The earliest golf courses were made in a circular pattern. The players would begin near the clubhouse and follow the holes around, finishing near where they started.

Q Why did wooden clubs once have twine wound tightly around the neck?

A The string, called "whipping," provided reinforcement and strength where the shaft and the club head came together, thus keeping the club from splitting and cracking. Today other materials have replaced the whipping.

Q Why are there dimples on a golf ball?

A Using the same aerodynamic principle that makes airplanes leave the ground, the dimples provide lift for the ball. Air is trapped by the tiny cups in a way that makes air move over the top of the ball more quickly than around the bottom. This causes the ball to rise.

Q Why do golfers yell "Fore!" to warn other players that a ball may be coming their way?

A This term probably originated during the sixteenth century with the British army, which formed ranks for battle by putting infantry at the front and artillery at the back. The artillery would yell "beware before" to the infantrymen before they fired; the infantry would then lie down to let the cannonballs pass over their heads.

golf

Q Why aren't golf tees made of something more durable than wood, which often breaks when the ball is hit?

A If tees were made of metal or plastic, they might damage wooden clubs. Also, wooden tees are inexpensive. But tradition might be the most important reason. It can be difficult to persuade most golfers to change their ways; many resist even switching over from white tees to colored tees.

Q After making a long putt, why do pros often let their caddies retrieve the ball from the cup?

A Caddies usually wear sneakers, not spiked shoes, so they can approach the hole without adding more spike marks to the green.

Q What does "warming the eggs" mean?

A Some pros ask their caddies to carry their golf balls in their pockets, believing that warm golf balls fly farther; however, it has not been proved that there is any truth to this belief.

Q How old must a player be to play on the Senior Tour?

A Senior Tour players must be at least fifty years old.

Q Is golf played in the Olympic Games?

A It was until 1904. In 1908, because of a dispute and an ensuing boycott, only one entrant showed up. Golf has not been part of the Olympics since.

Q What is a baffy?

A A baffy is the term used to describe the early version of a 4-wood.

Q If it rains during a tournament, can a caddie hold an umbrella over a pro while the pro is putting?

A No, the rules of golf state that "a player shall not accept physical assistance or protection from the elements." This rule ensures that no one player has an unfair advantage over another.

Q The U.S. Women's Open has been won by only one amateur. Who was she?

A Catherine LaCoste of France, who won in 1967.

Q Who was the first golfer to win the PGA Rookie of the Year Award?

A Ken Venturi.

Q What famous entertainer had a handicap as low as five or six?

A Bob Hope.

Q How many rounds does the average private-club golfer play in a year?

A About thirty-four rounds.

Q Who was the first professional golfer to amass $1 million in career earnings?

A The legendary Walter Hagen.

················▶ golf

Chapter 15

Even More
Quips and
Quotes

Surely the closest place to Heaven in all of sports is a golf course.

—*Frank Deford*

The reason the pro tells you to keep your head down is so you can't see him laughing.

—*Phyllis Diller*

There was a thunderous crack like cannon fire and suddenly I was lifted a foot and a half off the ground. . . . Damn, I thought to myself, this is a helluva penalty for slow play.

—*Lee Trevino, when lightning struck*

He enjoys that perfect peace, that peace beyond all understanding, which comes at its maximum only to the man who has given up golf.

—*P. G. Wodehouse*

golf

Now on the pot, Johnny Tee.
>   —*Los Angeles Open announcer,*
>   *mixing up his introduction*
>   *to Johnny Pott*

You've just one problem. You stand too close to the ball—after you've hit it.

>   —*Sam Snead,*
>   *giving advice to his pupil*

He took a swing like a man with a wasp under his shirt and his pants on fire, trying to impale a butterfly on the end of a scythe.

—*Paul Gallico*

If it weren't for golf, I'd probably be a caddie today.

—*George Archer*

golf

Sneaky little devil, Polts.
Thought he was just a terrible
player. . . . But he's laid a lawn
front and back of his new bunga-
low, entirely out of divots.

—*J. R. Coulson*

Never smash a club over your opponent's head. You can't replace it under the fourteen-club rule.

—*H. Thomson*

Every day I try to tell myself this is going to be fun today. I try to put myself in a great frame of mind before I go out—then I screw it up with the first shot.

—*Johnny Miller*

It was stupid. I learned a lesson. When you have to fight with a club, the club always wins.

—*Patti Hayes*

Real golfers, whatever the provocation, never strike a caddie with the driver. The sand wedge is far more effective.

—*Huxtable Pippey*

Hitting the ball is the fun part of it, but the fewer times you hit the ball the more fun you have.

> —*Lou Graham (on why golf is a dumb game)*

The best place to refine your swing is, of course, right out on the practice range. . . . You will have an opportunity to make the same mistakes over and over again so that you no longer have to think about them, and they become part of your game.

> —*Stephen Baker*

A wife always knows when her husband has had a bad round. He has pond weed in his socks.

—*P. Brown*

When they were awarding a car for a hole in one on a particular hole, I hit a 4-wood . . . and my ball bounced onto the hood of the car. Someone told me, "I don't think you understand. You have to hit the hole, not the car."

—*Mary Dwyer*

Never give up. If we give up in this game, we give up in life.

—*Tom Watson*

If this was a prizefight, they'd stop it.

—*Bob Hope*

golf

When miracles happen on the golf course, it is important to know how to respond to them. Songwriter Hoagy Carmichael, an avid golfer, once teed up on a par-3 hole, picked up a club, and hit the ball. It bounced once on the green, hit the pin, and dropped in for a hole in one. Hoagy didn't say a word, but took another ball from his pocket, teed up, then observed, "I think I've got the idea now."

—*Buddy Hackett*

The ball will hook toward the more dificult of two hazards.

—*Gary Kibble*

Golf is the most over-taught and least-learned human endeavor: If they taught sex the way they teach golf, the race would have died out years ago.

—*Jim Murray*

golf

I had a wonderful experience on the golf course today. I had a hole in nothing. Missed the ball and sank the divot.

—*Don Adams*

I'm not very good with a gun, but I'm hot with a wedge.

—*Anne-Marie Palli*

(on killing a duck that flew across the course)

My career started slowly and
then tapered off.

—*Gary McCord*

Only on days ending in *y*.

—*Jerry West*
(when asked how many days
a week he played golf)

Golf is a game whose aim is to
hit a very small ball into an even
smaller hole, with weapons singu-
larly ill designed for that purpose.

—*Winston Churchill*

golf

That putt was so good, I could feel the baby applaud.

—*Donna Horton-White*
(on making a twenty-five-foot putt
while seven months pregnant)

Titleist has offered me a big contract not to play its balls.

—*Bob Hope*

Give me golf clubs, the fresh air, and a beautiful partner, and you can keep my golf clubs and the fresh air.

—*Jack Benny*

I was three over: one over a house, one over a patio, and one over a swimming pool.

—*George Brett*

Be funny on a golf course? Do I kid my best friend's mother about her heart condition?

—*Phil Silvers*

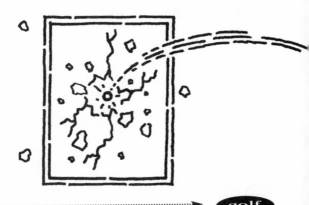

golf

Anything I want it to be. For instance, the hole right here is a par-47, and yesterday I birdied the sucker.

—*Willie Nelson*
(when asked what was par on
a Texas golf course he owns)

If you think it's hard to meet new people, try picking up the wrong golf ball.

—*Jack Lemmon*

At Jinja there is both hotel and golf course. The latter is, I believe, the only course in the world which posts a special rule that the player may remove his ball from hippopotamus footprints.

—*Evelyn Waugh*

My swing is so bad I look like a caveman killing his lunch.

—*Lee Trevino*

One of the remarkable things about Walter Hagen was the fact that, even in their defeat, his opponents all had tremendous affection for him.

—*Fred Corcoran*

The nice thing about these [golf] books is that they usually cancel each other out. One book tells you to keep your eye on the ball; the next says not to bother. Personally, in the crowd I play with, a better idea is to keep your eye on your partner.

—*Jim Murray*

It's nice to look down the fairway and see your mother on the left and your father on the right. You know that no matter whether you hook it or slice it, somebody is going to be there to kick it back in the fairway.

—*Larry Nelson*

golf

The fairways were so narrow you had to walk down them single file.

—*Sam Snead*

If you pick up a golfer and hold it close to your ear, like a conch shell, and listen, you will hear an alibi.

—*Fred Beck*

I remember he was so wild that when the word got out that he was taking a lesson, the parking lot was emptied of Cadillacs in five minutes.

—Max Elbin, golf pro (on President Richard Nixon)

Shoot a lower score than everybody else.

—Ben Hogan (on the secret of winning the U.S. Open)

I played as much golf as I could in North Dakota, but summer up there is pretty short. It usually falls on Tuesday.

—*Mike Morley*

However unlucky you may be, it really is not fair to expect your adversary's grief for your unde-served misfortunes to be as poignant as your own.

—*Horace Hutchinson*

Golf is a game in which you yell fore, shoot six, and write down five.

—Paul Harvey

They call it golf because all of the other four-letter words were taken.

—Raymond Floyd

A lot more people beat me now.
>   —*Dwight Eisenhower (on his*
>   *game after his presidency)*

Ninety percent of the putts that
fall short don't go in.
>   —*Yogi Berra*

Golf is the most fun you can have
without taking your clothes off.
>   —*Chi Chi Rodriguez*

I can airmail the ball, but sometimes I don't get the right address on it.

—*Jim Dent*

All I've got against golf is it takes you so far from the clubhouse.

—*Eric Linklater*

If there is any larceny in a man, golf will bring it out.

—*Paul Gallico*

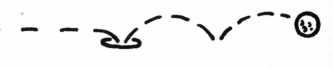

golf

If it really made sense to "let the club do the work," you'd just say, "Driver, wedge to the green, one-putt," and walk to the next tee.

—*Thomas Mulligan*

If you watch a game, it's fun. If you play it, it's recreation. If you work at it, it's golf.

—*Bob Hope*

410

Sometimes when I look down at that little white golf ball, I just wish it was moving.

—*Dusty Baker*

His driving is unbelievable. I don't go that far on my holidays.

—*Ian Baker-Finch, on John Daly*

The safest place would be in the fairway.

—*Joe Garagiola (on the best place for spectators to stand during celebrity golf tournaments)*

Find a man with both feet firmly on the ground and you've found a man about to make a difficult putt.

—Fletcher Knebel

The game of golf is not how many good shots you hit, it's how few bad shots you hit.

—Jack Nicklaus

The older you get, the easier it is to shoot your age.

—Jerry Barber

The only problem is that it's hell to find your way home every night.

—*Lee Trevino (on playing four different golf courses during the Bob Hope tournament)*

Chapter 16

Equipment from Spoons to Surlyn

Golf equipment has evolved through the years in a never-ending search for the perfect match between man and tool. Each new piece of equipment gives a golfer hope that it will magically transform his game.

In Ancient Days

A look at some of the rather primitive equipment of yesteryear on display in the museum of the Royal and Ancient Club of St. Andrews in Scotland and at the USGA museum in Far Hills, New Jersey, will make you wonder how those pioneer golfers managed to whack the ball with as much power and skill as the records show they did.

Early golf clubs weren't made to fit the individual. Tall men played with short clubs, often having to stoop to make contact. And when short men played with long clubs, it appeared the clubs were playing them!

Club grips were so bulky and slippery that players carried a product made of coal dust and applied it periodically when their hands became sweaty. Messy, but necessary.

In the early 1930s, Lawson Little, playing in the British Amateur, had so many clubs in his bag that his caddie asked to be paid extra. In 1934, the USGA passed a rule limiting the number of clubs carried to fourteen. The Royal and Ancient Golf Club, never an

organization to make impulsive
decisions, took until 1939 to pass
a similar rule.

Groovy!

A golf club has grooves on its
face, which keep the ball from
sliding up on impact. The grooves
on a club and the dimples on the
ball work together to help propel
the ball forward.

Gloves

Why do golfers wear only one
glove? Usually one hand (the left

for right-handers) has far more
contact when the club is gripped.
A glove on the other hand would
keep the hand from feeling and
controlling the club face.

Tee Off

The word tee probably comes
from the Scottish word *teay,*
which means a pile of sand.
Early golfers made a pile of sand
or dirt and placed the ball on top
for driving. The wooden tee
wasn't used until the early 1900s.

Battle of the Balls

The first golf balls were made of leather and stuffed with boiled goose feathers. It was no easy feat to stuff an entire bucket of feathers through a small hole. The best ball makers could only make about four balls a day. In wet weather, the balls became sodden and flew apart. In spite of the fact that a player seldom got more than two rounds from one "featherie," the game was played with this crude ball for nearly four centuries.

It wasn't until 1845 that the first gutta-percha ball was introduced. The legend goes that a professor at St. Andrews University received a statue of Vishnu wrapped in gutta-percha, a gummy substance made from tree sap. It occurred to him that he could roll this material into a good golf ball.

"Gutties" had a huge impact on golf. These rubber-like balls were easy to make, inexpensive, and durable.

In 1899, Coburn Haskell came up with a ball made from winding rubber thread under heavy tension around a solid rubber core. But golfers complained these balls were a little too lively around the greens. Haskell's balls earned the nickname "bounding billies."

In 1901, when Walter J. Travis displayed sensational putting with a Haskell ball and won the U.S. Amateur Championship, golfers took the new ball more seriously.

Over the years, materials substituted for the rubber core included a small sac of water, lead, zinc oxide, solutions involving glue, glycerin and water, and steel.

Modern balls are either three-piece or two-piece. Three-piece balls consist of a core wound with rubber and covered with balata, a soft gum from the bully tree. Balata balls are thought to offer better playability, meaning the golfer can shape his shot and get more action, or backspin, on the greens.

Two-pieced balls have a solid core and are usually covered with surlyn, a harder man-made material that resists cuts and nicks.

This ball doesn't produce as much spin as one covered with balata. However, it's less expensive and longer lasting, and it gets better distance. Take your pick!

There are 25 million golfers in the United States, but the industry sold 850 million golf balls in 1996. "That's a lot of water hazards," Jim Gorant, editor of *Popular Mechanics,* said to a Top-Flite employee. "Thank God," the employee responded, "it keeps us in business."

To Spike or Not to Spike
Metal spikes on golf shoes have
been around since at least 1914,
when a victorious Walter Hagen
swaggered off the eighteenth
green during the U.S. Open wearing a pair of "hob-nailed shoes."

A green-friendly alternative to
metal spikes is the tiny poly-
urethane disk, thought to be one
of the most significant equipment
introductions in the last thirty
years. Ernie Deacon, manager of a
golf club in Idaho, is the man

responsible for developing the idea of the plastic cleat in 1992.

Soft spikes were originally designed so fanatic golfers could play on damage-prone greens in the winter. Some of the earlier versions of plastic cleats had the nasty habit of popping out of shoes, so the original packets came with a tube of glue. Tammie Green became the first LPGA winner to wear plastic golf cleats.

Nearly 2,000 golf courses around the country have banned metal spikes. Most cite a desire for healthier fairways and smoother greens. If the trend continues, metal spikes may go the way of polyester pants.

Professionals disagree as to whether the new, green-friendly spikes are worthy. Many pros say they won't wear them because they change their game. Some consider slippage while wearing soft spikes to be a problem.

Others insist they're too conscious of them and that wearing soft spikes throws off their swing.

Meanwhile, shoe manufacturers are hustling to develop the perfect green-friendly golf shoes.

Golf Togs

Golfers have worn colorful clothing since the beginnings of the game. The idea of wearing bright colors in order to be seen while playing carried over from archers and the military wearing bright colors on their "playing" fields.

What are "plus fours"? This phrase refers to the knickers golfers used to wear. Four inches were added to the normal length of pants to create the bloused effect. In the 1920s, baggy plus fours in lightweight colorful fabric, matched with two-tone shoes and a sleeveless Argyle sweater and blazer, were a must for the well-dressed male golfer. During this period, women played in full-length skirts, hats, and high-buttoned blouses.

golf

Get a Grip

Before 1750, clubs had no grips at all; players simply held the bare wooden shaft. The first grips were plain cloth wrapped around the shaft. Later, silk, wool, and sheepskin were used. In the nineteenth century, leather became the grip of choice. By the 1950s, rubber grips were standard. Today, most grips are rubber or synthetic rubber.

The grip does more than keep a golfer's hands from slipping. The thickness and feel of the grip is very important. According to John Wheatley, expert on club-fitting and shaft technology, "You have to understand that a grip affects the club's flex, overall weight, and weight distribution."

Niblicks and Mashies

Early golf clubs were made of wood. The heads were glued to the shaft and bound with twine. Called niblick, brassie, spoon, mashie, and mashie-niblick, these clubs varied so much that the idea of a matched set of clubs was an impossibility.

Before long, some clubs began to be made with metal heads. Steel-shafted clubs were legalized by the United States Golf Association in 1924.

Modern-day woods usually have heads made of persimmon or maple, although more recently, some "woods" may have heads of metal.

The hot metal in today's clubs is titanium. It's 40 percent lighter than steel, stronger, and has excellent properties of flex and torque. Boron and graphite are also popular, but these advanced materials are expensive. Plain old steel shafts work just fine too.

Finding the right clubs can seem like a complicated business. Investment cast, lie-angle, cavity back—even the terminology is confusing. However, attention paid to the grip, the length of the shaft, and the materials used can make a big difference in how well a particular club suits a player. Some people get so involved in all the choices that they build their own clubs!

Bob Mendralla Sr., a club designer at Wilson for more than fifty years, says, "The overall weight of the club isn't what matters, it's how you distribute that weight. That's the key."

Equipment has evolved a lot over the years. Recalling his time as a club maker at the Homestead Resort in 1934, Sam Snead noted that wooden club shafts often used to get warped if they got wet or if they were left leaning against a wall, adding: "Sometimes you'd have to soak them in a barrel to get them to straighten out again."

Chapter 17

Etiquette, Customs, and Advice

Etiquette

Arrive at the course ten or fifteen minutes before your tee time. Be ready to play when it is your turn.

Make sure the players who are in front of you are out of range before you hit the ball.

Faster groups should be invited to play through. On some courses, management may have a different policy.

Don't damage the course when taking practice swings, especially around the tees.

Keep quiet and don't move when someone is addressing the ball or making a stroke.

When on the green, do your preparatory survey while others are putting if you can do it without distracting them.

golf

Unless otherwise specified, two-ball matches should be allowed to pass through three- or four-ball matches.

Mark your ball with a coin or ball marker if you don't plan to finish your putt at that time. Other players can suffer a 2-stroke penalty if they hit your ball.

Write your score down after reaching the next tee.

If a player loses the ball, determine quickly if a time-consuming search will be needed. If so, signal the group behind to play through, and then wait until they are out of range before you finish playing.

A group playing a whole round is entitled to play through a group playing a shorter round.

When everyone has finished playing a hole, immediately leave the putting green.

When using a cart, drop one player off at his or her ball with enough clubs to handle the shot. Then drive the second player to his or her ball.

Check around to be certain that your club won't hit anyone as you swing. Then check that no one will be hit by your ball, pebbles, or anything else that your club might propel.

If you're playing by yourself, everybody else can play through.

Refrain from scuffing your feet and gouging the green. Repair any damage you cause.

Don't step between a golfer and his line of putt. Your footprints can affect the roll of his ball.

Never leave your golf cart in the fairway while you putt.

Don't play a mulligan if a group is waiting behind you.

golf

Never leave your ball in the hole after you have finished putting.

Don't stand behind a player's line of hitting; it can be distracting.

When on the putting green, never lean on your putter when retrieving your ball—it can make an indentation on the green.

Compliment your partner and other players when they have made a good shot.

Replace divots.

Leave your beeper and cellular phone at home.

Help your partner locate his ball.

Be free with your compliments about other players.

Encourage a partner who is having a bad day.

Don't put your golf bag on the putting green.

Smooth over any holes or footprints you may have made in a bunker.

Always enter a bunker from the back, not from the front.

Don't take pull carts onto the putting green.

When you take the flagstick out of the hole, place it gently on the ground; do not throw it down.

Replace the flagstick in the hole when you have finished playing.

If you're the worst player in your group, don't delay play. As a courtesy to the rest of your group (as well as those behind you), pick up your ball if everyone else has long since finished and you are still playing.

If you are having a bad day—even if you are having a terrible day—don't whine and complain about it.

golf

Customs

In the "featherie" era, before the late 1800s, men playing golf wore red coats with swallowtails, sometimes accompanied by a top hat. But a man's everyday suit was also considered correct.

The British Open Championship trophy is a claret jug, because players gathered in early clubs to eat and drink claret as well as to play golf.

The custom of the captain of the Royal and Ancient Golf Club of St. Andrews having to "play himself in" developed in the mid-1700s. The first winner, John Rattray, won the silver club honor and was declared Captain of the Golf. Today, the captain of the club must "play himself in" by participating in the club's medal competition. He is considered the winner after his first stroke, and a cannon sounds to mark the victory. The caddie who retrieves the ball receives a gold sovereign.

Golf did not always have the eighteen-hole course that is customary today. Courses at Leith and Blackheath, Scotland, had five holes, and North Berwick and the London Scottish Volunteers on Wimbledon Common had seven. At one point, St. Andrews had twelve, which grew to twenty-two. In 1764, the Royal and Ancient Club at St. Andrews settled the number at eighteen.

The holes and greens that characterize golf courses might be attributed to sheep and rabbits. Course features could have been created by these first golf architects when the sheep nibbled grass, creating "greens," and rabbits scraped depressions in the turf, resulting in "holes."

"Scared head" clubs are named for the diagonal splice or "scare" used to attach wood heads to clubs.

By the nineteenth century, dress for golf was pretty much a matter of personal choice. However, most societies required players to wear red coats so they could be easily spotted on the course. The coats might have sported colored lapels or facings and silver or brass buttons inscribed with the club insignia or motto.

Greenskeeping developed to maintain courses when local club makers and professional golfers had less and less time to do it themselves.

454

Advice

Protect yourself from the sun: Wear a hat.

Put your name and address on your golf bag.

Don't play during an electrical storm. Lightning on a golf course can be extremely dangerous.

Be prepared: Bring an umbrella when you play.

When you are thinking of getting new clubs, try them out on a practice range first.

Bring extra tees and balls each time you play.

Try working as a volunteer at a golf tournament. You'll have fun, and you'll probably learn a lot too.

Always have a spare ball in your pocket.

Make sure the shoulder strap on your bag makes carrying your bag comfortable.

Clean your clubs after playing.

After a bad shot, laugh, and don't make excuses.

Join the USGA.

When it's too rainy to play, rent a video of golf instruction.

Save money and beat the crowds by playing at nonpeak hours.

Chapter 18

Celebrity Golfers

Kevin Costner

He once played the part of down-and-out golfer Roy McAvoy in the film *Tin Cup*. Costner loves the game and is an excellent player with a 13 handicap. At Pebble Beach in 1996, Costner was paired with Tiger Woods.

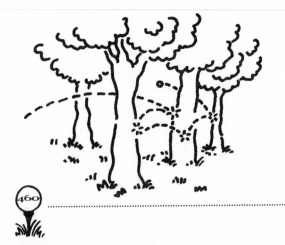

Arthur Conan Doyle

Arthur Conan Doyle, the author of the Sherlock Holmes legend, visited fellow writer Rudyard Kipling in Vermont in 1894 and introduced his fascinated host to the game of golf.

Ivan Lendl

The former tennis superstar plays a round of golf every day and has a 6 handicap.

golf

Sean Connery

Golf great Hale Irwin once said of Connery: "Sean has a presence to him and he carries that to the golf course." Connery is considered one of the better celebrity golfers, although he didn't take up the sport until he was thirty-five.

Clint Eastwood

Jack Lemmon tells a story about the day Clint Eastwood actually held him by the seat of his pants so he could make a golf shot on the sixteenth hole at Cypress Point. Lemmon hit his ball into an ice plant, two feet over the edge of a cliff where, in Lemmon's words, "there's a drop of eighty to one hundred feet, straight down to the ocean." At Eastwood's urging, Lemmon took the shot while Clint held onto his drawers. Lemmon's shot landed on the green.

golf

Ned Beatty

Beatty has teamed up with the Easter Seals Foundation to host the Ned Beatty Hope for Children Classic Golf and Tennis Tournament. In its second year, the tournament benefits disabled and disadvantaged children.

Jack Wagner

Ex–*General Hospital*er and current *Melrose Place* star Wagner took up the sport of golf at age ten. His teenage years were spent in expectation of becoming a professional golfer. He attended the University of Missouri for a year and won the state golf championship, then applied to the University of Arizona for a golf scholarship. He didn't get it. Undaunted, he auditioned for the drama program and won a full scholarship. The rest is history.

George Bush

Former president George Bush, an extremely enthusiastic golfer, comes from a serious golfing family. His father served as secretary for the USGA, and his grandfather, George Herbert Walker, donated the trophy for the Walker Cup.

Sylvester Stallone

Sly is often seen practicing his swing at the Studio City Golf driving range in Los Angeles. Stallone is known there for his intensity. He used to hit bucket after bucket of balls, day after day, until he felt he got it right. He is a member of the Sherwood Country Club, along with James Woods and Wayne Gretzky.

Oscar de la Hoya

In 1995, de la Hoya played a round of golf at the Spanish Trail in Las Vegas, just four days before his International Boxing Federation championship bout with Rafael Ruelas.

Huey Lewis

This rock-and-roll star is so infatuated with the game of golf that he named his fourth album *Fore*.

Rick Rhoden

Rhoden, the former Pittsburgh Pirates pitcher, won more than $500,000 playing in Celebrity Golf Association events.

Bob Clement

When Representative Bob Clement of Tennessee was invited to play a round of golf with President Bill Clinton, he had only a half hour's notice. He ran to buy $240 in sportswear so that he wouldn't have to play in his business suit, and borrowed some clubs from the prez. Clement admits that he isn't a great golfer. His first shot ricocheted off a tree and narrowly missed Clinton's head.

Dinah Shore

Dinah loved golf, and her memory is kept alive in the Nabisco Dinah Shore Championship. This tournament is referred to as the "Masters" of women's golf and is in its twenty-seventh year.

golf

Bing Crosby

Crosby, a passionate golfer who once had a handicap as low as 2, belonged to Lakeside Golf Club, in Toluca Lake, California, with such notables as Howard Hughes, Johnny Weismuller, Jean Harlow, and W. C. Fields. Crosby was the five-time club champ. On October 14, 1977, he died of a heart attack while playing golf in Spain.

Celine Dion

When Dion, the largest-selling
pop vocalist of 1997, started to
play golf, she set a ridiculous
goal of shooting a double-bogey
round of 108. She nearly made it
in just six weeks. Her husband
and manager, Rene Angelil, said
in a *Ladies Home Journal* article,
"She hits two
hundred and
fifty balls
every day."

Bill Gates

After Gates got married, he decided to take up golf. A close friend said that the computer guru has become a real golf addict, and that golf gets his "competitive juices" flowing.

Bob Goen

Goen has a hectic schedule as cohost of TV's popular *Entertainment Tonight*. Yet when he wants to relax, he's happy to go "any place that has a golf course."

Bill Clinton

President Clinton is a fair golfer, but it wasn't the golf course that caused his well-reported knee injury in 1997. Still, the disability did have a connection to golf. Clinton fell down pro golfer Greg Norman's back steps.

Howard Hughes

American industrialist, film producer, and aviator Howard Hughes was an extremely good golfer who once held a handicap of 1 stroke. Apparently, if Hughes had a bad day on the golf course, he would stay out long past dark, hitting balls by the light of movie floods.

Richard Riordan

The mayor of Los Angeles is a member of Los Angeles Country Club, but he is the only high-profile celebrity member. The L.A.C.C. denies membership to stars and high-powered notables in order to protect the privacy of its well-to-do members. In fact, Bing Crosby lived on the four-teenth fairway of the club, but could only play the course as a guest. Riordan joined before he decided to seek public office.

Donald Trump

When Trump was in the pit of his financial difficulty in 1990, he decided to take up golf again to help him relax and admitted in his book *Trump: The Art of the Comeback* (1997) that he won a great deal of money playing golf. In fact, he wrote that he once told golf great Jack Nicklaus, "You know, Jack, I've actually made much more money playing golf than you have."

Dean Martin

Before his death, Martin had become somewhat of a recluse. Yet his daily routine included a round of golf at the Riviera Country Club in Pacific Palisades, California. Martin also belonged to the Bel-Air Country Club, where James Garner, George C. Scott, Bob Newhart, and Glenn Campbell are members.

golf

Bill Murray

Murray loves to play golf and wishes he had more time for the game. His golf attire sometimes consists of cutoffs, a Hawaiian shirt, and a baseball cap. One thing everyone agrees on about Murray's game is that it needs a lot of improvement!

Bryant Gumbel

Gumbel, the former *Today Show* host, is often seen playing in celebrity tournaments. One of his regular golfing buddies is current *Today Show* host Matt Lauer.

Will Smith

Smith loves to golf. In 1995, he became a member of North Ranch, a country club in Westlake Village, just north of Los Angeles. Also a member is sixties rock-and-roll star Frankie Avalon.

golf

Stedman Graham

Businessman, former pro athlete, and significant other of Oprah Winfrey, Graham hosted a "Celebrity Golf Challenge" in 1996 to benefit the organization he founded, Athletes Against Drugs, and raised more than $50,000. Other participants in the tournament included baseball legend Ernie Banks, boxing champion Evander Holyfield, Olympic track and field medalist Willye White, and former Chicago Bulls star Craig Hodges.

Jack Lemmon

Lemmon, a member of the Golf Nuts Society, is listed in their roster as "the world's most frustrated golfer." But with a 21 handicap, how frustrated can he be? Lemmon has been trying to make the cut at Pebble Beach's Pro-Am for more than thirty years, to no avail. His favorite casual outfit is still a pair of slacks, a pastel golf sweater, and matching socks.

golf

Ronald Reagan

Although Reagan was diagnosed with Alzheimer's disease in 1994, he continues to play golf twice a week, sometimes with Tom Selleck and publisher Walter Annenberg.

Dan Marino

The Miami Dolphins quarterback recently joined the advisory board of the Celebrity Players Tour, and lends his name to the Dan Marino Invitational at Weston Hills Country Club in Fort Lauderdale, Florida. This pro-am event features celebrities such as Denver Broncos quarterback John Elway, baseball greats Mike Schmidt and Johnny Bench, and the rock singer Meatloaf.

George Clooney

Each year, Clooney takes a group of seven actors and industry people that he calls "the boys" with him on vacation. Most of them are people he met making such flops as *Red Surf, Return of the Killer Tomatoes,* and fifteen series pilots before he finally hit it big with *ER*. Several years ago, he flew all of "the boys" to Acapulco for Christmas. In 1996, they rented a bus and made a golfing tour of the Southwest.

Sugar Ray Leonard

Sugar Ray plays at Riviera Golf Club in Los Angeles. Some of his fellow club members include Stephen Bochco and Peter Falk.

golf

Bob Hope

With a handicap that was once
as low as 5 or 6, Hope has
played golf all over the world
with sports figures and celebrities
of every distinction. This popular
entertainer was inducted into the
World Golf Hall of Fame in
1983, and lends his name to the
Bob Hope Chrysler Classic.

Dwight Eisenhower

Both during and after his presidency, Eisenhower played golf as often as he could and even had a green installed on the White House lawn. He claimed that his happiest moment came when, at the age of seventy-seven, he hit a hole in one on the thirteenth (par-3) hole at the Seven Lakes Country Club in Palm Springs. He called it "the thrill of a lifetime."

Chapter 19

Rules of
the Links

The Honourable Company of Edinburgh Golfers compiled the original list of thirteen rules of golf in 1744. Today, the *Official Rules of Golf,* as approved by the United States Golf Association and the Royal and Ancient Golf Club of St. Andrews, Scotland, fills more than a hundred pages. This makes it appear that golf is a complicated game, which it really is not.

Gary McCord, in his book *Golf for Dummies,* suggests keeping in mind the following basic tenets:

Play the course as you find it.

Play the ball as it lies.

If you can't do either of those things, do what's fair.

golf

However, special cases in golf constantly arise, and players and spectators alike should benefit from reading through the *Official Rules of Golf*. Some of the most important rules can be summarized as follows:

Carry no more than fourteen clubs.

Be sure there is some kind of identification on your ball. If you can't tell whether a ball is yours or not, it's lost.

On the first tee, the honor (who hits first) is determined by the order of the draw or by lot. Play the ball from a spot not more than two club lengths behind the tee markers.

In match play, the ball farthest from the hole is played first. The side that wins a hole shall have the honor at the next hole. In stroke play, the ball farthest from the hole is played first. The player with the lowest score tees off first at the next hole.

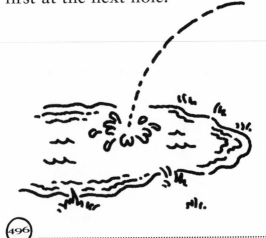

Play the ball as it lies. Don't improve your lie by moving anything fixed or growing that may be in the way. If your ball lies in a hazard, don't touch the hazard with your club before you hit the ball.

If you lose your ball in a water hazard, you can drop another ball behind the hazard at the point where the ball first crossed the hazard, but you must take a 1-stroke penalty.

Obstructions are man-made, artificial objects that are not part of the course and that do not define out of bounds. If they are movable, you may move them. If they are not (fences, roads, etc.), you may drop within one club length of your nearest relief (but not nearer the hole) without penalty.

Loose impediments are natural objects such as leaves, twigs, stones, etc., and may be removed if it can be done without moving the ball, unless the loose impediment and the ball are in a hazard.

If you lose your ball anywhere else but in a hazard, or if you hit your ball out of bounds, return to where you hit your previous shot and hit another, with a 1-stroke penalty.

If your ball is unplayable, you may play from where you hit your last shot, drop within two club lengths of where your ball is now (but not nearer the hole), or drop any distance behind the point where the ball lies (keeping that point directly between the hole and the spot on which the ball is dropped). In all cases, you must take a 1-stroke penalty.

When putting, make sure you take the pin out of the hole, since you risk a penalty if your putt hits the pin.

Always hit the ball into the hole ("hole out") unless your opponent concedes your putt.

golf

Chapter 20

Not the
Hole
Truth

When Duffer McPutt asked for yet another day off—this time to attend a cousin's funeral—his boss replied, "If only you would give the same attention to your work that you do to your golf game." Duffer looked horrified. "Good heavens, sir, I could never be that serious about my work."

Excerpt from a North Carolina state publicity brochure: ". . . famous mid-south resorts, including Pinehurst and Southern Pines, where it is said that there are more golf curses per square mile than anywhere else in the world . . ."

Bluffer: Did you hear that they've just done a survey to find out the height of the average golfer?

Duffer: No, what did they learn?

Bluffer: That the average golfer is not as tall as his stories.

- - - - - - - - -

Overheard: one frugal Scot to another:

"Great Scott, ye've holed in one!"

"Ay, it saves wear an' tear on the ball."

golf

One Saturday, a huge rainstorm hit just as two golfers finished the eleventh hole. They ran to shelter under a maple tree.

"How'd you do on that last hole?" asked one of the golfers, shaking water out of her hair.

"Four," replied the other golfer.

Just then, there was an enormous clap of thunder, and a bolt of lightning lit up the sky.

"On second thought," said the golfer, "change that to a six."

After losing yet another ball, the visitor threw his club to the ground in disgust. He turned to his caddie.

"I have never played on a course like this in my whole life," he sputtered.

"But sir," said the caddie with a grin, "you haven't been playing on the course for the last thirty minutes. The course is half a mile to the west."

Tony: I heard you made it around the course in 82.
Tim: Heavens, no. I wasn't even born in '82.

Little Timmy accompanied his father one Sunday on his weekly round of golf. He watched in silence for the first nine holes. Then he tugged on his father's arm and asked, "Why do you work so hard to keep the ball out of those little holes?"

Not the Hole Truth

Just as a golfer was about hit his drive off the seventh tee, a woman wearing a wedding dress came running across the course.

"You slime!" she cried. "You no-good liar. How could you do this to me?"

The man drew back his club and hit a long ball straight down the fairway. Then he turned to the woman." I never lied to you," he said. "I said, 'Only if it's raining.'"

It was midafternoon on the fourteenth tee. Just as a foursome was preparing to tee off, a man rushed over from the thirteenth green. "Excuse me," he said to the closest member of the foursome, "but could I possibly play through? I've just gotten word that my wife has been taken quite ill."

The weekend golfer, dressed in bright plaid slacks and brand new golf shoes, turned to his caddie on the eighteenth hole and asked smugly, "So what do you think of my game?"

The caddie shrugged. "I suppose it's all right. But I prefer golf."

golf

You don't love me at all," cried Jill. "I'll bet you don't even remember the day we met."

"Of course I remember that day," said Will. "It was the day I got a birdie on the twelfth hole."

Gladys marched into the house and threw her scorecard down on the kitchen table in despair.

"That's the last straw," she said to her husband. "I'm never going to play this game again as long as I live."

"Why, what happened?" asked her husband.

"I lost a ball on the back nine. Then I lost a ball on the front nine. And then . . . " Gladys put her head into her hands. "I lost a ball in the washer."

A duffer was playing a round of golf on Sunday afternoon. The duffer's caddie was disgusted by the poor play of his employer, and his frustration was growing. The duffer eyed the distance to the next green and asked the caddie, "Do you think I can get there with a 5-iron?" The caddie answered, "Eventually."

Belinda leaned across the table and said, "I'll never play golf with Nancy again. She cheats."

"Really?" said Marge. "How do you know?"

"Because she hit a ball out of the bunker that disappeared into the rough. We looked for it and looked for it, but we couldn't find it. Then all of a sudden, there it was, right next to the green. I tell you, she cheats."

"How do you know it wasn't her ball?" asked Marge.

"Because," said Belinda, "I had her ball in my pocket."

Molly: I wish I knew what to do to stop topping all my drives.

    Polly: Why don't you try turning the ball upside down?

Duncan came home after a day on the golf course, not realizing that his son, Freddie, had returned home just before him.

"How did it go?" asked his wife, greeting him at the door. "Freddie said he spent the whole day as your caddie."

"Why, so he did!" said Duncan. "I thought there was something familiar about that boy."

Tom and Don were playing a round of golf one day, when all of a sudden Don had a heart attack and died, right on the seventh fairway. Later that afternoon, when Tom was telling some friends back in the clubhouse what had happened, they said, "Oh my, that must have been terrible."

"It was," said Tom. "For the rest of the day, it was hit the ball, drag Don, hit the ball, drag Don . . ."

Two women were just starting on the back nine when a funeral procession passed by on the road next to the course. The first player stopped and stood at attention until the hearse had passed. "That was a nice gesture," said the second player. The first player replied, "It seemed the least I could do. After all, we've been married for almost thirty years."

Player to his caddie: Why do you keep looking at your watch?

Caddie: It isn't a watch, it's a compass.

A young couple expecting their first child was talking with their obstetrician. The doctor, who was discussing the importance of exercise, turned to the man and said, "It would be a good thing if you were to get out and walk with your wife." The man responded, "How would it be if she carried a bag of golf clubs while walking?"

Chapter 21

Believe It or Not

A company in Japan is working to develop a biodegradable golf tee that would turn into compost in a matter of hours. Such a tee would mean an end to golf courses littered with lost and broken tees.

There is so much golfing traffic on the Fukuoka Golf Course in Japan that stoplights have been placed at three holes.

526

A woman from Pennsylvania holds the record for the highest score ever achieved for a single hole. Most of her strokes were made from a rowboat as she followed her floating ball down a stream. (This was over eighty years ago, when golf balls still floated.) Her total: 166!

Long ago, before lawn mowers came into being, sheep were used to keep the grass on the greens cut short.

golf

The youngest player on record to score a hole in one in the United States was Coby Orr, in 1975. He was five years old at the time, and was playing on the Riverside Golf Course in San Antonio, Texas. In Britain, a six-year-old named Mark Alexander had a hole in one in 1989 at Chessington, Surrey. The youngest girl to hit a hole in one was six-year-old Brittny Andreas, who hit a hole in one in Austin, Texas, in 1991.

Those who play at the Nyanza Club in British East Africa may play another ball without penalty if their first ball lands too near a crocodile or a hippopotamus.

D. J. Bayly MacArthur once attempted to play out of a sand trap in Australia—only to discover it was quicksand. He had sunk in up to his armpits by the time someone came along to help.

When Ian Baker-Finch, who won the British Open in 1991, won the Bridgestone/Aso Open in Japan two years earlier, he was quite surprised to learn that his prize included a cow.

In 1939, an unlucky golfer named McFarland swung his club in disgust. The club flew out of his hand and killed his caddie.

Geoff Howson wrote a book titled *How to Look Good When You're Not,* in which he figures out that during an average round of golf only 4.097 percent of playing time is spent actually hitting the ball.

Niles Lied, an Australian, drove a golf ball across an ice cap at Mawson Base in Antarctica in 1962. The total yardage: 2,640 yards, or one and a half miles.

Astronaut Alan B. Shepard is said to have been inspired by Bob Hope when he brought a 6-iron with a four-piece aluminum shaft to the Moon in 1971. He placed two balls on the lunar surface and hit them. Because of the space suit he was wearing, it was difficult for him to make a proper pivot on the swing. Furthermore, he had to hit the ball with just one hand. The 6-iron he used is now on display in the USGA's museum in Far Hills, New Jersey.

While playing at St. Anne's Golf Course in Scotland, Aubrey Boomer accidentally hit the ball straight up in the air. When the ball came down, it landed right in his pocket.

A ball that flies out of bounds, hits a billboard, and bounces back onto the course is considered still in play.

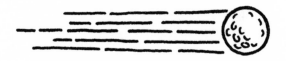

golf

During World War II, the St. Mellons Golf and Country Club in England posted the following rules:

- Players are asked to collect bomb and shrapnel splinters found on the course.

- In competition, during gunfire, or while bombs are falling, players may take shelter without penalty for ceasing play.

- A ball moved by enemy action may be replaced, or if lost or destroyed, a ball may be dropped without penalty, not nearer the hole.

- A player whose stroke is affected by the explosion of a bomb may play another ball under penalty of 1 stroke.

Just before the Masters of 1958, Frank Philips, an Australian golfer, killed a black-snake he encountered in the woods along Augusta National's sixth green. He placed the dead snake in the hole. Soon after, Mike Souchak sank his putt, only to find a snake curled around his ball when he went to retrieve it from the cup.

Dinah Oxley, member of the British Curtis Cup teams of 1968 and 1970, once hit a drive that veered off the course and onto a nearby road, shattering the windshield of an oncoming car. The driver, James Henson, pulled to the side of the road and was invited into the clubhouse to recover. Dinah and James became friends—and eventually married!

 A Scottish player called Tony Green used to go golfing with his golden retriever, Ben. One day after a round of golf, Ben appeared to be extremely ill. Tony called the vet, who decided on emergency surgery—and discovered that Ben had swallowed eleven golf balls! The dog recovered, but he was never invited to play golf with his master again.

Ky Laffoon supposedly tied his putter to the back of his car and dragged it down the road to punish it for its failings.

While playing in the 1990 Australian Open, Bret Ogle managed to lodge his ball behind a tree. He used a 2-iron to try to slide past the tree, but the ball ricocheted off the trunk and flew into his leg, breaking his kneecap.

If a robin perches on the iron marker of the hole you are playing, bad luck may be coming.

Mark O'Meara traveled to Los Angeles to play in the 1995 Nissan Open, only to discover that he could not play because he had failed to enter.

Bent grass, a fine-bladed turf grass, is considered to be the best kind of grass for greens, since it can be mowed as low as one-eighth of an inch in height.

Bobby Locke is said to have taken his putter to bed with him.

When Wendy Ward was playing in an LPGA event in West Palm Beach in 1998, she accepted a ride in a cart between holes, which was in violation of the rules. The result: a 2-stroke penalty. She lost the tournament by five strokes, so the penalty didn't affect the outcome of the match.

golf

A herd of young bulls were spending their days in a field adjacent to the Headingly golf course near Leeds. When one of the bulls began losing a great deal of weight, it was slaughtered. To everyone's amazement, fifty-six golf balls were discovered in its stomach.

The three golf courses at Kapalua on Maui are certified by the Audubon Society as Audubon Cooperative Sanctuaries.

The Palm Beach Invitational became the first PGA tournament to make a major donation to charity—$10,000 in 1938.

Billy Joe Patton, playing as an amateur in the 1954 Masters, amazed the world by hitting a hole in one, which propelled him to a second-place finish.

In two consecutive rounds at the 1986 Chrysler Classic, Arnold Palmer aced the seventh hole.

golf

Chapter 22

Golf

Disasters

Palmer's Fumble at the U.S. Open

One of the most infamous golf disasters in history is attributed to Arnold Palmer during the 1966 U.S. Open. Holding seven major titles, Palmer took a 3-stroke lead into the final round at Olympic in San Francisco. With a front-nine 32, he managed to build that lead to a whopping seven strokes. Palmer then collapsed completely, dropping to a 39—which tied him with Billy Casper, who shot a brilliant 32 on the back nine that day. Palmer then lost the tournament by four strokes to Casper in the next day's play-off. Though he never won another major title, Palmer's positive attitude after the loss was proof of great sportsmanship; extraordinary support by fans and family after his disaster helped him cope and move ahead. "You have to put it behind you," he said, "if you want to win again."

Norman's Disaster at the Masters

Greg Norman, 1995 PGA Player of the Year, was off to a brilliant start at the 1996 Masters. His first round, a 63, matched the course record and set a record for the tournament's opening round. The spectators went wild with enthusiasm when he remained the leader after the second and the third round as well. During the fourth round, however, Norman's game went badly awry. Later admitting he had lost his timing, Norman ran into trouble again and again between the tenth and fifteenth holes. Nick Faldo was able to erase a 6-stroke deficit and go on to win the tournament. Norman's last-round score was a heartbreaking 78.

Sheehan Done in by Exhaustion

In 1990, Patty Sheehan was favored to win the 1990 U.S. Women's Open. By the end of the tournament she would prove to the golf world the importance of a good night's sleep and a healthy breakfast.

During heavy rains at the Atlanta Athletic Club, Sheehan played late into the evening on Saturday. Up early on Sunday to play the final rounds, she didn't eat much before heading out with her clubs. Still, she led by nine giant strokes with twenty-seven holes to play. Then exhaustion and dehydration set in and wrestled with her ability to think clearly. Her lead broke down to 4 in the final round, then to 2. At this point, Sheehan missed a twenty-foot birdie putt at the eighteenth hole to lose to Betsy King. It seems she learned her lesson, however. Water bottle by her side, she won consecutive Opens in 1993 and 1994.

Player Plays It Wrong

In 1955, on his first trip to Britain, the young Gary Player played in a small tournament in Huddersfield. At the last hole, he was told he needed a 4 to win. Desperate for a victory, he drove the ball with determination, but unfortunately he hooked it, and it landed right up against a stone wall. Player figured his only chance for the 4 was to bounce the ball off the wall and onto the green. He hit the ball as planned, but it ricocheted off the wall and hit him in the chin, knocking him out cold.

When he recovered, he chipped onto the green and holed his putt, thinking, in his dizzy state, that he had the winning 4. Unfortunately, he forgot to take into account the 2-stroke penalty incurred when the ball struck his chin. Even worse, he soon learned that a 5 would have won him the tournament after all. Had he known this, he would have played the hole very differently.

Sneed's Stumble at the Masters

In 1979, it was Augusta National's back nine that tripped up Ed Sneed and would begin his plummet off-course for the Masters title. Opening with rounds of 68-67-69, Sneed took a 5-stroke lead into the final round. He surprised himself, his fans, and his opponents as he bogeyed on the way home to set up the first sudden death play-off in Masters history with a final round of 76. Fuzzy Zoeller made a six-foot putt for a birdie on the second extra hole to win.

Sneed has said that this loss in no way had a negative effect on his game, that in fact the media portrayed it as much more devastating than it really was. "I just had a chance to win and I didn't," he said. Forging ahead, Sneed went on to win one more title on that tour, the 1982 Houston Open. He retired in 1984 with a back injury.

Snead's Most Bitter Loss

Though Sam Snead never won a U.S. Open, he did have a number of chances. In June of 1939, at the seventy-first hole on the Spring Mill course of the Philadelphia Country Club, it seemed that he had won the title. Perhaps over-confident, Snead three-putted the hole. He needed a par-5 on the next hole to win, a bogey to tie. His historically beautiful swing landed the ball in the rough.

He didn't know how his

opponents Craig Wood and
Denny Shute were doing behind
him, but he figured that he probably needed a birdie. He figured
wrong, topped the shot, and sent
the ball into a bunker about 110
yards short of the green. Then he
added salt to the wound by lodg-
ing it between cracks of freshly
laid sod. He freed it with a chop,
sending it into another bunker,
then shot it forty feet past the
hole. He three-putted for a score
of eight. He finished the game
two strokes behind Byron
Nelson, Wood, and Shute.

Morgan Falls Out of the Race

Gil Morgan was forty-five years old when he had a good chance to win his first major title. With twenty-nine holes left, Morgan led by seven strokes in the 1992 U.S. Open. Then, his luck appeared to run out, and he ended up with a score of 9 over par over the next 7 holes. He ended the day tied for the lead, but the worst was yet to come. The following day, the would-be champion played a final round of 81. He again tied for his position, but this time it was for unlucky thirteenth. "I kind of fell out of the sky," he said later. "It felt like my parachute had a hole in it."

Trouble on the Green for Green

It was 1978, and Hubert Green, the confident hopeful for the Masters title, was at his best. Having won the 1977 U.S. Open, he came into the tournament thinking he could whip everyone. Everything seemed to be going his way, too, as he led by three strokes into the final round. Costly mistakes at the eleventh and sixteenth holes were followed by catastrophe at the eighteenth, where he fell apart, sliding a three-foot birdie effort right by the hole. Green tied for second place as Gary Player closed the game with a record-tying 64.

Still confident, and competitive to the end, Green commented that he played as well as anyone else and just wished Player had missed his last putt. He did his best to put that day behind him, seemingly successfully, since he went on to win the PGA Championship in 1985.

Hogan's Fall at the U.S. Open

In 1948, Hogan won eleven tournaments, including the U.S. Open and the PGA title. Having barely survived a car crash a couple of years later, he made what doctors called a miraculous recovery. Somehow, he won three National Championships in 1953 and stepped onto the Olympic course in the 1955 U.S. Open tournament at peak performance. His goal: to be the first person to win the U.S. title five times.

Before the last holes had even been played, reporters gave Hogan national congratulations for attaining his goal. However, Jack Fleck, a self-taught golfer, was behind him playing the game of his life. Fleck made a birdie on the eighteenth to tie with Hogan.

Everyone still expected Hogan to win the play-off. On the final hole Hogan hit his tee shot into the rough and shot a 6. Fleck two-putted for a solid par and won by three solid strokes to become the Open champion.

Stephenson's Loss at Baltusrol

Jan Stephenson hoped to make golf history in the 1985 U.S. Women's Open not by winning but by changing an official rule during the game. She played confidently on the Baltusrol course in New Jersey and was tied for the lead at the turn in the first round. On the eleventh green her birdie putt was a little short. No big deal; she marked the spot with a dime and patted it down with her putter. Unfortunately for her, an

LPGA official saw the coin stick to her putter, then fall off. He cited a rule whereby if a player is involved in the moving of a ball marker, she is dealt a 1-stroke penalty. Stephenson argued and fought the rule, but to no avail. The incident had upset her game. She faltered throughout the rest of the tournament and lost the title. Apparently the golf world took a look at this rule and today a player is not penalized if a marker moves; the player simply replaces it.

Burns and the Slingshot Shot

University of Maryland player George Burns badly shanked his second shot when playing against Penn State. His ball flew over the perimeter fence in the general direction of the local railway. Just as Burns shook his head in disappointment and started to turn away, the flying ball hit a telephone wire. The wire, acting like a giant slingshot, stretched and stretched and then propelled

the ball back onto the course.
Burns was amazed to see the ball
not only roll onto the green but
stop a mere six feet from the
hole. He was so undone by the
whole affair that he then twelve-
putted the hole.

Chapter 23

Words to
the Wise

Eat, drink, and be merry, for tomorrow you may go off your game again.

If at first you don't succeed, try looking at the ball.

If at first you do succeed, try to hide your astonishment.

He who has the fastest cart seldom has a bad lie.

Words to the Wise

I once gave up golf—it was the
most terrifying hour of my life.

The older I get, the better my
golf game used to be.

Missing! Golfer-husband and
dog, not seen since Saturday
morning: reward for dog.

Golfers come and golfers go, but mostly they go.

If all the golfers in the world were laid end to end, they would lie indefinitely.

If you see two people talking and one of them is yawning and looking at her watch, the other one is the golfer.

If you swing your club like an ax, don't be surprised when you strike a tree.

If golf is for the rich, as some people say, then why are there are so many poor players?

Old golfers don't die—they just lose their drive.

Chapter 24

Golf

Terminology

A

Address: To take a stance in preparation of hitting the ball.

American ball: A golf ball with a weight not more than 1.62 ounces and a diameter not less than 1.68 inches, as specified by the United States Golf Association.

Apron: The narrow strip of grass surrounding the putting green that is cut shorter than the fairway, but not as close as the green itself.

Away: The ball or player that lies

farthest away from the hole and is to be played next.

B

Back: The last nine holes of an eighteen-hole course; a teeing ground that is at the farthest spot away from the hole, so that the hole is played at its greatest distance.

Backspin: When the ball rotates backward during its flight.

Backstroke: When a player swings the club backward and

up, to the point where it begins
to move down again; backswing.

Balata: Substance derived from the
gum of the balata tree that is used
to cover rubber-cored golf balls.

Banana ball: Slang for a bad slice.

Bank shot: When the ball is
pitched onto the face of a steep
bank so that it goes over on the
bounce.

Barranca: A ravine or watercourse that is typically rocky and incorporated into some golf courses as a hazard.

Baseball grip: Grip style where the hands are placed together without overlapping or interlocking.

Bend: To hit the ball so that it has a sidespin, which makes the shot curve; the curve of a shot due to sidespin.

Bent: A type of grass commonly used on greens.

Best ball: The lowest score of a two-man partnership, playing in a foursome, on a single hole.

Birdie: A score of 1 under par for one hole.

Bite: The backspin that causes a pitched ball to land on the ground and stop dead or nearly so or even pull back.

Blade: Part of an iron club head where the ball is hit; to hit the ball on the leading edge of an iron club head.

Blind: The part of a hole, green, or hazard that is hidden from the player's sight; to play a ball into the hidden part of the hole, green, or hazard.

Block: To stop wrist rotation during the swing and cause the ball to be sliced because the club face did not close to square upon impact.

Bogey: A score of 1 over par for one hole.

Bulger: Any wooden club (usually a driver) with a slightly convex face.

Bunker: An area of sand or a sandpit on a golf course that is sometimes edged by embankments and used as a hazard; to play into a bunker.

Bye: Holes that remain to be played when a match is won before the eighteenth hole.

C

Caddie or caddy: A person who carries the golfer's clubs; to do the work of a caddie.

Carpet: A term used in golf to refer to the fairway or the putting green.

Charge: To play or putt with bold strokes; to have success playing the course aggressively; a dramatic surge of excellent play from a player who was lagging; to surge dramatically from behind in play.

Chili-dip: To hit the ground before hitting the ball.

Chip: A shot that is short and moderately lofted with little back-spin; to hit a chip shot.

Chip in: Holing out with a chip

shot; any chip shot that holes out.

Chip-and-run: A chip shot and its run after landing; to make a chip-and-run shot.

Choke: To grip the club far down the shaft; to become nervous during play.

Cleek: A wooden-shafted club, narrow-bladed and light, used for chip shots.

Come back: To putt again after having putted past the cup.

Come out: To shoot from a bunker.

Compression: The amount of flexibility in a golf ball.

Cross-handed: When a right-handed player grips the club with the left hand below the right; when a left-handed player grips the club with the right hand below the left.

Cut: Backspin, often with a slice; a method by which the field of competitors in a tournament is reduced; the score by which players are eliminated from competition.

D

Dead: When the ball stops so close to the hole that the next putt will sink it; when the ball falls from flight without rolling.

Deuce: A hole in two.

Die: When a putted ball stops rolling.

Divot: The piece of turf that is sliced from the ground by the head of a golf club as it makes a stroke; the hole left by this action.

Dogleg: A sharp turn in the fairway; a hole that has such a turn.

Dormie: In match play, when the number of holes up equals the number of holes that remain to be played.

Double-bogey: A score of 2 over par for one hole.

Double-eagle: A score of 3 under par for one hole.

Draw: A shot made by a right-handed player that starts out straight and then moves to the left; or a shot made by a left-handed player that moves the ball to the right.

Drive: To shoot from the tee with a driver, using full power; to play from a tee.

Drive-and-pitch: Description of a hole where the green can be reached with a combination of a drive and a pitch.

Driver: A long-hitting wooden club, such as the number 1 wood. *Driving iron:* Another name for the number 1 iron.

Drop: To drop a ball onto the course during play, such as when the ball is unplayable or lost; to hole out a putt.

Duck-hook: When the shot of a right-handed player flies low and curves sharply to the left and down; when the shot of a left-handed player flies low and curves sharply to the right and down.

Duff: A bad swing that hits the ground behind the ball first, then tops the ball.

Duffer: An unskilled golfer.

E

Eagle: A score of 2 under par for one hole.

Eight-iron: An iron club, also known as a pitching niblick; any shot made with an 8-iron.

F

Face: The part of the club head with which the ball is struck; the striking surface of a club.

Fairway: The stretch of open

grass that extends from the tee to the green.

Fairway wood: Any wooden club that is effective on the fairway; any wooden club, other than the driver; a shot played with a fairway wood.

Five-iron: An iron club, once known as a mashie; any shot made with a 5-iron.

Five-wood: A wooden club; any shot made with a 5-wood.

Flat: When the angle of a club is relatively wide between the head and the shaft; when a swing moves horizontally.

Flip or flip shot: Any approach shot that is hit briefly and gently with a high-lofted iron, and achieves a high trajectory.

Fly: When the shot plays clear over a hazard, a green, or other feature of the hole; a high shot;

to land from flight without bouncing.

Follow-through: The act of swinging the club after making contact with the ball.

Foozle: A poor shot.

Fore: What a player calls when people on the course are in danger of being hit by his ball.

Form: The manner in which a player plays; a player's style of play.

Four-iron: An iron club that is also known as a mashie-iron; any shot made with a 4-iron.

Four-wood: A wooden club that is also known as a spoon; any shot made with a 4-wood.

Fried-egg: A ball that is half-buried in the sand.

Front: The first nine holes of an eighteen-hole course.

G

Gallery: The group of spectators at a golf tournament.

Gateway: Part of the fairway that leads up to the green, particularly when hills or hazards lie on both sides.

Gimme: A putt that is so close to the hole that it is conceded without the player actually putting the ball.

Globe: A whiff; a stroke that fails to hit the ball.

Gobble: A putt that is hit hard and holes out.

Grain: The direction in which blades of grass on a putting green lie.

Greenside: The area beside the putting green.

Grip: The part of the club that the player holds; the way a player holds the club.

Groove: Scored lines on the face of a club.

Gutta-percha: Sap of several Malaysian trees from which golf balls were made from the mid–nineteenth century until the beginning of the twentieth century; made from gutta-percha.

H

Hack: To play golf poorly; to hit the ball with violent, crude strokes.

Hacker: An untrained player.

Handicap: An allowance of strokes assigned to a player based on his or her history of play, which allows players of different abilities to compete on somewhat equal terms.

Hazard: An obstruction or difficult part of a golf course, such as a sand trap or water.

Head: Club head; the part of the club with which the ball is struck, usually made from wood, iron, or steel.

 ....

Golf Terminology

Heel: The part of the club that lies immediately below the neck; to hit a ball from the heel of the club.

Hole in one: A hole completed in one stroke.

Hole out: To putt the ball into the hole.

Hook: A ball hit by a player that curves in flight to the left; to hit any such shot.

Hosel: The neck of an iron club

head; to strike the ball with the hosel.

I

Iron: Any club with a head that is made from iron or steel.

J

Jerk: When the ball is played from the sand, the rough, or a bad lie, with a downward cut so that the club head digs into the ground beneath the ball before impact; a shot that is jerked.

L

Lag: To putt just short of the hole.

Lay back: To tilt the face of the club back in order to increase its loft.

Lay up: To make a shorter shot than could be made, to avoid a bad lie or a hazard.

Lie: The position of the ball as it sits on the course; the angle between the shaft of the club and the horizontal when the club is in the correct position for address.

Loft: To play the ball so that it makes a steep trajectory; the angle that a club is laid back from vertical; the angle between the club face and the shaft.

Lofted: When there is a somewhat steep loft in the face of the club.

Loose impediments: Natural obstructions that aren't part of the course, that may be removed without penalty, except when found in hazards.

M

Mulligan: Not according to strict rules, permission for a player to replay a bad shot, usually a tee shot.

N

Nassau: A three-part bet on a golf round covering the first nine holes, the last nine holes, and the entire round, with each part carrying an equal wager.

Nine-iron: An iron club; any shot played with a 9-iron.

Nineteenth hole: The clubhouse bar.

O

One up: Having scored one hole more than an opponent in a match; a player who is one up; being in a position of advantage.

One-iron: An iron club; any shot played with a 1-iron.

P

Pair: Two partners in stroke competition or in a match; to combine two players who will act as partners in stroke competition or in a match.

Par: The standard number of strokes that it should take a superior golfer to complete a hole in clement conditions with no mistakes, based on one, two, or three strokes through the green plus two putts, depending on the length of the hole.

Peg: Tee.

Pin: Pole to which the flag is attached for marking the hole.

Pitch: To hit the ball so that it will have a steep trajectory, usually with significant backspin.

Pitch-and-run: A pitch (or chip) with a significant roll along the ground.

Pitching wedge: An iron club usually used for pitching shots onto the green; any shot made with a pitching wedge.

Press: To overdo a stroke; to put too much force into a stroke; an extra bet made during the game.

Putt: Gentle stroke made with the putter, usually on the putting green, in anticipation of sinking the ball into the hole.

Putt out: To hole out with a putt.

Putter: Club designed for putting that is usually straight-faced, nearly upright, and usually short-shafted.

Q

Quarter shot: Shot made with an underpowered swing; shot made with half the force of a half-shot.

R

Relief: Permission to lift and drop the ball that is sanctioned by the rules under certain conditions and carries no penalty.

Reverse overlap: Grip of a right-handed player whereby the forefinger of the left hand overlaps the little finger of the right; grip of a left-handed player whereby the forefinger of the right hand overlaps the little finger of the left.

Rim out: When the ball circles the rim of the cup but does not fall into the hole.

Rough: Area of the course where the ground cover is much higher than the fairway.

S

Sand iron: Sand wedge.

Sand wedge: Club used for playing out of the sand; any shot

played with a sand wedge.
Scramble: To play unevenly.

Scratch: A handicap of zero.

Seven-iron: An iron club; any shot made with a 7-iron.

Shaft: The long part of the club enclosed by the grip at the top, ending at the clubhead below; made primarily from tubular steel.

Shank: When the ball is hit with the hosel of an iron club.

Short: Not close to the objective; to hit the ball a shorter distance than intended.

Single: A match in which only two players participate.

Slice: A ball, hit by a player that curves in flight to the right; to hit any such shot.

Sole plate: The metal plate attached to a wooden club head with screws.

Square: When the match stands even with both sides winning the same number of holes; a stance in which both feet are parallel to the line of play.

Stance: The golfer's position when addressing the ball.

Straightaway: A straight fairway.

Sudden death: In case of a tie, a play-off in which the first to win a hole wins the match or the tournament.

Supinate: When the wrist is rolled so that the palm of the hand faces upward.

Sweet spot: The place to hit the ball on the club face that will produce the best result.

Swing: Movement of the arms and legs that constitutes a golf stroke, composed of the backswing, the downswing, and the follow-through.

T

Takeaway: The backswing.

Tee: Any raised mound of dirt, sand, or other device on which the ball is placed in preparation for driving; a clearly marked area from which the first shot of a hole is hit.

Tee off: To play a shot from the tee.

Tee up: To place a golf ball on a tee.

Three-iron: An iron club; any shot made with a 3-iron.

Threesome: A type of match in which one player is pitted against a two-player side and, where members of the two-player side alternate in playing one ball.

Three-wood: A wooden club; any shot made with a 3-wood.

Toe: The end of a club head that is farthest from the shaft; to hit the ball with the end of the club head that is farthest from the shaft; to turn the club toward the player's feet.

Torque: The degree to which the shaft of the club twists under the pressure of hitting the ball.

Tour: A series of tournaments in which professional golfers compete.

Two-iron: An iron club; any shot that is made with a 2-iron.

Two-putt: To play the green in two putts.

Two-shot: When a hole requires a drive and another shot to make the green.

Two-shotter: A two-shot hole.

Two-wood: A wooden club; any shot made with a 2-wood.

U

Unplayable: When the lie of the ball is so difficult to play that the player opts for relief and penalty under the rules.

Upswing: The backswing.

V

Vardon grip: Overlapping grip.

W

Waggle: A preparatory wave of the club over and behind the ball at address; to perform the waggle before making a stroke.

Wedge: Pitching or sand wedge; 10-iron; any shot made with a wedge.

Whiff: To miss the ball entirely when making a stroke; any stroke that misses the ball.

Wood: Any club with a heavy bulbous head, originally made of wood and now made of wood or metal.

Y

Yardage: The length of a hole or course.

Yips: A nervous affliction that causes difficulty in putting.

May your balls, as they fly
and whiz through the air
Knock down the blue devils,
dull sorrow and care.
May your health be preserved,
with strength active and bold,
Long traverse the green, and
forget to grow old.

—*Henry Callendar*
(secretary to the Royal Blackheath
Club, and its captain in 1790,
1801, and 1807)